the french cuisine I love

the french cuisine I love

by JULES J. BOND

LEON AMIEL • PUBLISHER
NEW YORK

Table of Contents

LIST OF COLOR PLATES

Published by
LEON AMIEL • PUBLISHER
NEW YORK
ISBN 0-8148-0677-5
©Copyright 1977, by Leon Amiel • Publisher
Printed in the United States of America

Foreword

Many people have visions of truffles and goose liver and of other delightful and expensive foods, or of rich sauces and complicated procedures, when they think of French food. True, many of those are the delight of gourmets, but the average French do not indulge in them too often.

The true glory of French cooking is the "Cuisine Bourgeoise," or as Curnonsky, the "Prince of French Gastronomes" called it, "La cuisine de nos mamans."

This book contains recipes of good French home cooking, dishes of the many regional cuisines of France.

They are chosen to be followed quite easily. Some have been simplified and adapted to available American ingredients. Some are party fare and some for the enjoyment of the family.

Bon appetit!

Jules Bond

Jules Bond

Sauce Mornay
(3 cups)

3 egg yolks, slightly beaten
¼ cup heavy cream
2 cups hot Béchamel sauce

2 tbsp. butter
2 tbsp. grated Swiss cheese
1 tbsp. grated Parmesan

Mix eggs with cream, then blend with hot Béchamel and cook over very low heat or in the top of a double boiler over simmering water, until the sauce reaches the simmering point. Do not let come to a boil. Add the grated cheeses and blend well.

Marchand de Vin Butter
(for 2 - to be served with broiled steaks)

2 shallots, minced
¾ cup dry red wine
1 tsp. meat glaze
  (or Bovril)

4 tbsp. butter, soft
freshly ground black pepper
2 tbsp. parsley, minced
juice of 1 lemon

Put shallots and wine in a small saucepan and cook until wine has almost evaporated. Then stir in the meat glaze and the pepper and swirl in the butter. When serving add the minced parsley and the lemon juice.

Sauce Béchamel

(about 2 cups)

2 tbsp. butter
1 tbsp. onion, minced
4 tbsp. flour
3 cups milk, scalded

½ tsp. salt
pinch of white pepper
1 sprig parsley
pinch of grated nutmeg

Melt the butter and sauté the onion until soft. Do not let onion take on color. Then add the flour, stir well and cook the roux gently, stirring constantly, for a few minutes until it just barely starts to take on color. Gradually add the milk, cook while beating with a wire whisk until the sauce is thick and smooth. Add parsley and seasonings. Simmer slowly for half an hour, stirring occasionally until sauce has reduced to two thirds of the original volume. Strain through a fine sieve.

Sauce Raifort
(Horseradish Sauce)
(about 1 cup)

4 tbsp. fresh horseradish, grated

1 tsp. lemon juice

salt and white pepper to taste

½ cup crème fraîche *(see page 20)* or heavy cream, whipped stiff

Blend well and serve with boiled hot or cold meats or poached fish. Bottled horseradish can be used in a pinch, but the taste won't be quite as satisfactory. When using bottled horseradish, drain well before measuring and omit the lemon juice.

Sauce Ravigotte
(about 4 servings)

2 tbsp. minced parsley

2 tbsp. chopped watercress

1 tbsp. minced chives

1 tbsp. minced fresh tarragon (or 1 tsp. dried)

1 tbsp. minced fresh chervil (or 1 tsp. dried)

2 anchovy filets, chopped

1 shallot, minced

1 tbsp. capers, drained and chopped

1½ tbsp. cornichons (or sour gherkins) minced

6 tbsp. olive oil

1 tbsp. wine vinegar

2 tsp. lemon juice

salt and pepper to taste

This should be a fairly thick sauce, to be served with boiled, hot or cold meats.

Blend all ingredients.

Sauce Beurre Blanc
(Butter Sauce)
(1 cup)

1½ tbsp. shallots, minced as fine as possible
4 tbsp. white wine vinegar
4 tbsp. dry white wine
8 tbsp. butter
salt and pepper to taste

Put shallots, vinegar and wine in a saucepan and simmer until the shallots are so soft that they have almost disintegrated and the liquid is reduced to not quite two tablespoons. Cool the liquid. Place pan over low heat and add the butter, one tablespoon at a time, whisking vigorously with a wire whisk, while the butter starts to melt. When the butter has just about melted, remove from the fire and keep whisking. The sauce should have the consistency of heavy cream. Season with salt and pepper and serve immediately over hot poached fish.

This is one of the great sauces, to be served with sole, salmon, trout or any delicate fish. While deceptively simple, a few unsuccessful tries in the beginning are almost unavoidable. But the end result is well worth the effort.

Sauce Remoulade

(2½ cups - served with cold fish or shellfish)

2 cups mayonnaise

2 tbsp. capers,
   drained and minced

2 tbsp. sour pickles, minced
   (French cornichons preferred)

1 tbsp. onion, grated

1 to 2 tbsp. Dijon mustard
   (according to taste)

½ tsp. anchovy paste

2 tsp. each of minced fresh
   parsley, tarragon, chervil
   (1 tsp. each if dried herbs)

Blend all ingredients well.

Sauce Verte

(about 1 cup)

10 spinach leaves, well washed

¼ cup watercress leaves

¼ cup parsley leaves (without stems)

1 cup mayonnaise

Blanch leaves in boiling salted water for 1 minute. Let stand for another minute, drain well and press out all water. Cool and rub through a fine sieve. Blend with mayonnaise. This very attractive and tasty sauce should be served with cold poached fish or shellfish, such as salmon, bass or lobster.

Sauce Bordelaise

(for about 1 cup)

½ cup good quality red
　　Bordeaux wine
5 shallots, finely minced
½ clove garlic, minced
cayenne pepper to taste
1 small bay leaf
3 tbsp. butter

salt and crushed pepper to taste
1 tbsp. meat extract
　　(Bovril or similar)
1 tbsp. cognac
¼ lb. beef marrow, poached
　　(ask your butcher for
　　the marrow)

Simmer shallots and garlic in wine, add cayenne, bay leaf, salt and pepper and cook until reduced to half its volume. The sauce should be fairly thick. Add cognac and meat extract, blend, bring to a boil again. Remove pan from heat. To make the sauce smooth and shiny, swirl in the butter in small pieces. Do not stir it in, just incorporate with a swirling motion. Poach marrow in boiling water for 2 minutes, then cut in rounds and add to the sauce just before serving.

Vinaigrette Sauce
(French Dressing)

The only real "French dressing" is the vinaigrette, a simple basic oil and vinegar dressing. The variations are numerous.

4 tbsp. oil
2 tbsp. wine vinegar
1 tsp. salt

¼ tbsp. freshly ground pepper
½ tsp. Dijon mustard
touch of crushed garlic (opt.)

Blend well.

Vinaigrette Sauce
(To be served with hors d'oeuvres)

4 tbsp. vinegar
½ tsp. dry mustard
8 tbsp. olive oil
1 tsp. chives, minced
1 tsp. parsley, minced
pinch of chervil

pinch of tarragon
1 tbsp. capers, squeezed
   dry and chopped
1 tsp. grated onion
1 hard-cooked egg, chopped
salt and pepper

Mix mustard with vinegar, add the herbs, onion, salt and pepper, blend well, then add oil and egg.

Sauce Piquante

For roast or grilled pork, boiled beef or braised tongue. This recipe is a shortcut using meat glaze instead of a sauce espagnol.

¾ cup dry white wine
¾ cup white wine vinegar
2 tbsp. chopped shallots
1½ tbsp. meat glaze
   (Bovril or similar)

1 tbsp. sour gherkins or
   French cornichons, minced
2 tbsp. of mixed fresh tarragon,
   chives, parsley
salt and pepper to taste

Boil wine, vinegar and shallots over high heat until reduced by half. Add the meat glaze and simmer for 10 minutes. Remove from heat, stir in the pickles and herbs, season with salt and pepper.

Court Bouillon
(for fish and shellfish)

1 cup dry white wine
4 cups water or fish stock
2 carrots
3 pieces of root parsley
2 shallots
2 medium onions

2 stalks celery
1 tsp. salt
½ tsp. dried thyme
½ bay leaf
6 peppercorns

Peel all vegetables and slice them thin. Put them in a kettle, along with all other ingredients and simmer until the vegetables are cooked soft. Then strain the liquid.

Note: If the court bouillon is to be used to cook shellfish, use wine vinegar instead of the white wine.

Fritter Batter
(3 cups)

1¾ cups sifted all-purpose
   flour
1 tsp. salt
1 tbsp. cooking oil

1 whole egg
²/₃ cup flat beer
¾ cup milk
2 eggs, separated

Beat together the flour, salt, oil, egg yolks and whole egg. Add the beer and milk and beat with a wire whisk or beater until the batter is smooth and fairly thick. Fold in beaten egg whites. Let rest for 15 minutes before using.

Aioli
(Garlic Mayonnaise)
(about 3 cups)

5 large cloves garlic
1 tsp. salt
3 tbsp. soft white
   breadcrumbs
3 egg yolks

white pepper to taste
1 tsp. Dijon mustard
2¼ cups olive oil
2 tbsp. wine vinegar

Crush the garlic with salt until reduced to smooth paste. Soak breadcrumbs in a little milk, squeeze out the milk and add crumbs to garlic paste. Add pepper and egg yolks, blend well and when the mixture is smooth blend in the vinegar and mustard with a wire whisk. Then begin adding oil, drop by drop, just as if making a mayonnaise. When mixture starts to thicken, pour oil in a thin stream. Correct seasoning and finish by beating in a tablespoon or two of boiling water, to improve the consistency. The finished aioli is thicker than a normal mayonnaise. It is a perfect sauce to serve with fish, cold meats and vegetables.

Beurre Manié

One of the easiest and best ways to thicken sauces. Knead equal amounts of butter and flour until smooth. Stir blended mixture into the sauce in small pellets.

Bouquet Garni

A combination of herbs added to stews, soups and stocks for flavoring. Most frequently used combinations are thyme, bay leaf and parsley. Tie fresh sprigs of herbs together with string. If dried herbs are used, tie in a cheesecloth bag for easy removal.

Duck à la Vasco da Gama — See page 86 for recipe.➔

Sauce Gribiche

(3 cups ~ Ideal with cold fish or shellfish)

6 hard-cooked egg yolks
1 tbsp. Dijon mustard
1 tsp. salt
freshly ground pepper
2 cups olive or salad oil
3 tbsp. wine vinegar

1 tbsp. fresh tarragon, minced
1 tbsp. parsley, minced
2 tbsp. capers, chopped
1 tbsp. sour pickles, minced
3 hard-cooked egg whites, minced

Mash the egg yolks until smooth. Then blend in the mustard, salt and pepper. Add the oil, little by little in the beginning, as though you were making a mayonnaise. As the mixture thickens, add some vinegar from time to time. When the oil is used up, blend in all other ingredients, and finally a spoonful of boiling water. This will insure a smooth, stable mixture.

←*Onion Soup* — See page 21 for recipe.

Crème Fraîche

In most French cookbooks one finds recipes calling for use of double crème or crème fraîche. American heavy cream is considerably thinner than French heavy crème, the crème fraîche. French cream is allowed to mature and ferment naturally, which gives it a much thicker consistency, and a slightly nutty, acid flavor. There is a very simple way to approximate the crème fraîche.

To each cup of heavy cream add one teaspoon of buttermilk. Blend, heat in a saucepan until lukewarm, about 85 degrees. Pour it into a glass or porcelain container and let it stand at room temperature until the mixture thickens, which can take anywhere from 6 to 36 hours, depending on the room temperature. Then store in refrigerator. Crème fraîche will keep for a week or more.

Onion Soup
(for 8)

6 medium sized onions,
minced
2 tbsp. cooking oil
6 tbsp. butter
3 tbsp. flour
8 cups hot chicken broth

salt and pepper to taste
French bread, sliced and
toasted
grated Swiss or Parmesan
cheese
cayenne pepper to taste

Combine oil and butter and sauté onions gently until they turn golden. Sprinkle the flour over onions and cook them, stirring constantly until they are light brown. Stir in the hot broth and simmer 15 minutes; season to taste with salt and pepper. Put soup in serving bowls or plates, put a few slices of toast in each plate, sprinkle liberally with grated cheese, add cayenne if desired and brown quickly under the broiler.

Billi Bi
(Cream of Mussel Soup)
(for 4)

1½ quarts mussels
1 medium onion, sliced
1 carrot, pared, sliced
1 stalk celery, cut in
   pieces
2 cups water
½ cup clam juice
½ cup dry white wine

8 tbsp. butter
¼ cup flour
salt and white pepper
   to taste
2 egg yolks
⅓ cup dry sherry
1 cup light cream
minced parsley and chives

Scrub the mussels under running water. Put them in a kettle, add onion, carrot and celery, water, clam juice and wine. Cover, bring to a boil and cook for about 5 minutes until the shells have opened. Remove from fire. Discard any mussels that have not opened. Shell the mussels, remove the beards. Strain the liquid through a cheesecloth, and reserve, along with mussels. Melt 6 tablespoons butter in a saucepan, stir in the flour, blend and then add the strained stock. Blend well again and bring to a boil over gentle heat. Season with salt and pepper. Force half the mussels through a coarse sieve or chop fine and add to the soup. Beat egg yolks with the sherry, then blend with the scalded light cream, add 2 tablespoons butter, dilute with some of the hot soup, mix and return the mixture to the soup. Stir well, add the mussels. Sprinkle with parsley and chives before serving. This soup is equally good hot or cold.

Potage Parmentier
(Leek and Potato Soup)
(for 6)

6 medium sized leeks
1 cup onion, chopped
2 tbsp. butter
4 large potatoes, peeled
   and diced
salt and pepper to taste

2 cups chicken broth
3 cups water
¼ tsp. grated nutmeg
2 cups milk
1 egg yolk
½ cup light cream

Trim green tops and roots off the leeks, split lengthwise in half and wash well under running water. Chop them coarsely. Melt butter in a heavy kettle, add leeks and onion, cover and cook slowly for 5 minutes until softened. Do not brown. Add potatoes, broth and water, salt, pepper and nutmeg, cover and cook for about 45 minutes until potatoes are very soft. Put soup and vegetables through a foodmill or use a food processor, return to kettle and heat to a simmer. Beat egg yolk with light cream, add slowly a cup of hot soup to the cream, blend well and then stir this mixture into the soup. Add milk, heat through, let simmer for a few minutes but do not let boil. Correct seasoning.

Garlic Soup with Poached Eggs
(for 4)

8 cups water
1¼ cups olive oil
8 cloves garlic, peeled
   and crushed
bouquet garni (small bay
   leaf, thyme, rosemary
   and sage)

1 tbsp. parsley, minced
8 eggs
8 slices French bread,
   toasted
salt and pepper to taste

    Put water in a saucepan, add oil, garlic, bouquet garni, parsley, salt and pepper. Boil for 20 minutes. Poach the eggs in this liquid, one or two at a time. Remove them with a slotted spoon, trim them neatly and keep warm. When serving, put two pieces of toast in each soup plate, put eggs on top and fill the plate with the soup.

Cream Soup Quimper
(for 6)

2 quarts mussels, well
  scrubbed
2 dozen steamer clams
¾ cup dry white wine
1 tbsp. shallots, minced
1½ cups leeks, white part,
  chopped fine
4 tbsp. parsley, minced
4 tbsp. butter

pinch of thyme
small bay leaf
pinch of cayenne pepper
pepper to taste
2 egg yolks
1½ cups crème fraîche
  (see page 20)
  or heavy cream
shellfish broth

Put shellfish in a saucepan, add wine, shallots, leeks, parsley, thyme, bay leaf, butter, cayenne pepper and pepper. Bring to a boil, cover and cook until shellfish have opened. Remove from fire, discard any clams or mussels that have not opened. Remove meat from shells, remove beards from mussels. Reserve shellfish. Strain the broth through cheesecloth, cool and reserve. Beat egg yolks until creamy, blend with the cream. Then add, while whisking, one cup of the broth. Blend well and mix with the remaining broth. Return to saucepan, add shellfish, heat through but do not let boil. Correct seasoning before serving.

Cotriade of Mackerel
(A Breton Fish Soup)
(for 6)

3 tbsp. butter

3 tbsp. cooking oil

½ lb. mushrooms, sliced

1 shallot, minced

5 medium leeks, white part only, minced

4 medium white onions, sliced thin

5 tbsp. flour

3 cups water

3 cups dry white wine

1 bouquet garni (parsley, bay leaf and thyme)

salt and pepper

3 cloves garlic, minced

juice of one lemon

6 mackerel filets, each halved

6 slices French bread, toasted

3 tbsp. parsley, minced

Heat half the butter and half the oil in a skillet and gently saute mushrooms, shallot and the white part of 1 leek for about 10 minutes in the covered skillet. Stir a few times. Heat remaining butter and oil in a heavy enameled saucepan, add onions and the remaining leeks, cover and cook over low heat until soft. Stir in flour and cook, stirring, for 2 or 3 minutes longer. Then add the mushroom mixture, water, wine and the bouquet garni, season with salt and pepper. Cover and cook over low heat for 15 minutes. Add garlic and lemon juice, mix well and add the mackerel filets. Cook over low heat for 10 to 15 minutes. Then transfer filets carefully to a hot platter. Correct seasoning of the soup, reduce quickly if desired. Discard bouquet garni. Put toast slices in the bottom of a tureen or serving bowl, pour the soup over the toast. Sprinkle parsley over the filets and serve them separately.

Petite Marmite
(for 6)

1 lb. beef shoulder, cut into 6 large cubes

1 2½ lb. chicken, cut in 8 pieces

8 cups beef broth

4 carrots, trimmed into 1 inch long pieces

2 white turnips, trimmed like the carrots

3 medium leeks, white part only, cut in 1 inch lengths

1 cup green cabbage, cut in chunks

3 stalks celery, white part only, cut in 1 inch lengths

1 parsnip, peeled and cut in 1 inch pieces

½ tsp. dried thyme

3 sprigs parsley

1 bay leaf

salt and pepper to taste

finely chopped chives

Put beef and chicken in a stock pot or deep saucepan, cover with about 4 cups of water, bring to a boil and simmer for 2 minutes. Drain off the water and discard. Rinse the meat and chicken quickly in cold water and return beef only to pot. Add the beef broth and 2 cups of water and simmer, uncovered, for 1 hour. Add chicken, vegetables, thyme, parsley, bay leaf, salt and pepper. Simmer for about one more hour or until chicken and vegetables are tender. Skim fat off top. Serve in soup plates, one beef cube, one piece of chicken and some of all vegetables in each plate. Sprinkle with chives before serving.

Soupe au Pistou

(for 8)

This is the famous soup of Nice — its ingredients and name no doubt influenced by the great sauce of neighboring Italy — the pesto.

1 lb. green snap beans
4 large potatoes
2 quarts water
salt and pepper to taste
4 tomatoes, peeled, seeded
   and chopped
1 cup dried haricot beans

4 small zucchini, cut
   into large dice
1 cup fine noodles, broken up
½ cup firmly packed fresh
   basil leaves
3 cloves garlic
¼ cup olive oil

Blanch haricot beans in boiling water for 2 minutes, then cool in same water for an hour. Drain. Trim the green beans and cut them in 1 inch pieces. Peel and dice potatoes. Bring water in a kettle to the boiling point, add green beans, potatoes, salt and pepper. Bring to a boil again, cover and simmer for 10 minutes. Add the haricot beans and tomatoes, let the soup boil up again and then simmer for about 45 minutes or until haricot beans are nearly tender. Add the zucchini and 3 or 4 minutes later the noodles. In the meantime pound the basil leaves and garlic, together with a little salt in a mortar to make a smooth paste, adding oil, a little at a time. When sauce becomes more liquid use a wire whisk instead of the pestle. The mixture should have the consistency of soft butter. Put this mixture in the soup tureen or bowl, stir in first a little of the soup, blend, and then add rest of the soup, correct seasoning and serve piping hot.

Garbure Bearnaise

This is more than a soup, it is the national dish all through the Pyrenées, and often the main meal of the day. And if you do as the Basques do, have a glass of red wine with the soup and stir a few spoonfuls into the soup before you start eating.

2 lbs. pork butt or smoked ham
3 quarts water
1 lb. dried white beans
1 onion, stuck with 4 cloves
1 lb. fresh or frozen
   lima beans
3 carrots, chopped fine
1 turnip, chopped fine
3 leeks, white and green
   part, chopped fine
1 medium cabbage, coarsely
   chopped

1 whole head garlic, unpeeled
2 hot peppers, fresh or dried
salt
2 cups coarsely chopped
   pumpkin or squash
3 potatoes, peeled and cut
   into large dice
3 tbsp. fresh basil, chopped
2 tbsp. fresh dill, chopped

Blanch dried beans for 2 minutes in boiling water, then let stand in the water for one hour. Drain. Put ham or pork in cold water, bring to a boil and drain. Put the blanched meat in a deep kettle with 3 quarts of water, bring to a boil and add the blanched dried beans. Then add onion, lima beans, carrots, turnip, leeks and cabbage, the whole head of garlic and the hot peppers. Season with salt and bring to quick boil. Let boil rapidly for 5 minutes, then reduce heat and simmer for about 1½ hours. After the first hour add the pumpkin, potatoes, basil and dill. Before serving remove garlic head and hot peppers. Correct seasoning. The Garbure should be quite reduced and very thick with vegetables when served. Cut meat in pieces and return to the soup.

Cold Vichyssoise Antoine
(for 8)

9 tbsp. sweet butter
½ lb. leeks, white part only,
   washed and chopped
1 cup thinly sliced white
   onion
½ cup canned sorrel leaves
   (drained) or 1½ cup
   fresh sorrel leaves
6 cups chicken broth*

2 large potatoes, peeled and
   diced
pinch of dried tarragon
small pinch of thyme
pinch of cayenne pepper
salt and white pepper
   to taste
2 cups heavy cream
4 tbsp. chives, chopped fine

   Melt butter in a saucepan, add the leeks and onions, cover and simmer for 20 minutes. Then add the sorrel, simmer a few minutes longer, add chicken broth, potatoes, tarragon, thyme, cayenne, salt and pepper and simmer covered for about one hour, until vegetables are very soft. Strain all through a fine sieve and force vegetables through it, or use a food processor with the steel blade or puree in a blender. Return to saucepan, and simmer again for 15 minutes. Then add the cream, bring to a simmer. Cool, correct seasoning and chill until ice cold. When serving, sprinkle chives on top of soup.

   *There are some very good brands of canned chicken broth available.

Pâté Maison

1 lb. lean veal, ground
1 lb. pork belly (fat pork),
   ground
½ lb. pork liver, ground
½ cup pork fat, diced small
1 large clove garlic,
   crushed
6 black peppercorns and
6 juniper berries, pounded
   in a mortar

salt to taste
pinch of mace
pinch of nutmeg
pinch of allspice
pinch of powdered ginger
⅓ cup dry white wine
2 tbsp. cognac
a few strips of thin
   pork fat

Blend all ingredients well, except the strips of pork fat. Let stand for a couple of hours. Then put into a one-quart terrine or deep casserole, arrange fat strips on top, put dish in a pan half-filled with hot water and cook in preheated 325⁰ oven for about 1½ hours. The sides of the paté will pull away from the dish when the paté is cooked. Do not remove fat from top of the paté. Cool completely. When fat has set, refrigerate overnight before serving.

Terrine of Chicken
(for 8)

3 cups cooked chicken meat
 (or turkey or duck), diced
½ lb. cooked ham,
 diced fine
1 lb. sausage meat
2 eggs
pinch of nutmeg
pinch of allspice
pinch of powdered ginger

1 tsp. chervil
1 tbsp. parsley, minced
2 shallots, minced
2 cloves garlic, crushed
4 tbsp. butter, softened
5 tbsp. brandy
salt and coarsely ground
 pepper to taste
½ lb. lean bacon

Mix sausage meat, ham, eggs, spices, chervil, shallots and garlic, butter, salt and pepper and brandy. Blend well. Line a terrine or casserole, 1½ quart size, with bacon strips, reserving a few strips. Add a layer of the sausage mixture, then a layer of diced chicken, and continue until all ingredients are used up. Spread the sausage mixture as a top layer. Then cover with the remaining bacon strips, cover the dish and place in a pan half filled with water. Bake in preheated 375° oven for 2 hours. Chill well overnight before serving.

Terrine of Pork and Veal
(for 8)

2 lbs. lean pork
2 lbs. shoulder of veal
  (boneless)
2 tsp. salt
pepper to taste
½ tsp. allspice (ground)
¼ tsp. mace

1 pinch powdered ginger
1 large carrot, peeled and
  chopped
1 onion, stuck with 4 whole
  cloves
2 cups dry white wine
2 envelopes unflavored gelatin

Put meats in a pot with cold water and bring to a boil. Drain, rinse meat under running cold water. Return meats and all other ingredients except gelatin to the pot, add water to cover and simmer over low heat about 2 hours. Remove the meat and chop it coarsely. Boil the broth until it is reduced to 4 cups, then strain through a fine strainer. Return the liquid to the pot, add the chopped meat and simmer for 15 minutes. Correct the seasoning. Soften the gelatin in a little cold water, add it to the kettle and mix well. Rinse a 2-quart mold with cold water, pour meat and broth into it and chill until well set. Unmold and cut into slices. Garnish with fresh parsley.

Terrine of Ham
(for 4)

½ lb. boiled ham
6 tbsp. butter
¾ cup crème Fraîche
  (p. 20) or heavy cream
2 envelopes unflavored gelatin
¾ cup chicken broth
½ cup dry Madeira wine
  (Sercial)

¾ cup chicken broth
2 tbsp. cognac
pinch of thyme
pinch of nutmeg
1 tsp. lemon juice
salt and pepper to taste
2 tbsp. parsley, minced

Put ham through meat grinder or chop fine in a food processor. Mix with softened butter until well blended. Then stir cream, thyme, nutmeg and lemon juice into the mixture. Soften gelatin in madeira and dissolve in hot chicken broth. Cool and add together with brandy, salt and pepper to the ham mixture. Blend well, pack into a mold and refrigerate until well set. Sprinkle with parsley before serving.

Steak Tartare — See page 98 for recipe.→

Ham Mousse

(for 6)

½ lb. cooked ham
8 tbsp. butter
1 cup heavy cream
salt and pepper to taste
pinch of dried thyme
2 tbsp. pimento,
     diced small

pinch of mace
2 envelopes unflavored gelatin
½ cup Madeira wine
     (Sercial)
1 cup chicken broth
¼ cup armagnac or cognac

Grind ham with the finest blade of the grinder or use a food processor, then blend well with softened butter. Blend in cream, salt and pepper, thyme, mace, and pimento. Bring the chicken broth to a boil, soften the gelatin in Madeira and then add to and dissolve in the hot broth. Cool the broth, blend in with the ham mixture, then add the cognac, blend once more. Correct the seasoning, pack into a mold and refrigerate.

←*Shoulder of Lamb Landaise*—See page 99 for recipe.

Poultry Liver Mousse
(for 6)

½ lb. chicken livers (or duck or turkey livers)
5 tbsp. cooking oil
⅓ cup onions, minced
4 shallots, minced
1 clove garlic, minced
pinch of mace
small pinch of allspice
small pinch powdered ginger
pinch of dry thyme
1 bay leaf
salt and pepper to taste
8 tbsp. butter
1 cup heavy cream
¼ cup cognac
1 envelope plain gelatin

Saute livers in oil over high flame for 4 minutes. Then add onions, garlic, shallots, spices and herbs and season with salt and pepper. Cook another 3 minutes. Remove bay leaf and discard. Force everything else through a fine sieve or place in the bowl of a food processor and chop fine with the steel blade. Blend in the butter, then the heavy cream. Soften gelatin in a tablespoon of cold water, then dissolve in a couple of spoonfuls of hot water, add gelatin and cognac to liver mixture, blend again and pack in a mold. Refrigerate well.

Salade Niçoise
(for 6)

Romaine or Boston lettuce
   leaves
2½ cups cooked green beans,
   cut in half
2½ cups cooked waxy potatoes,
   diced
2 cups canned tunafish,
   drained and broken into
   chunks

5 hard cooked eggs, cut
   in wedges
10 anchovy filets
½ cup black olives, pitted
½ cup green olives, pitted
strips of canned pimento
parsley, minced
3 tomatoes, peeled and cut
   into wedges

Dressing: Mix well:
1 tsp. Dijon mustard
½ tsp. dry mustard
salt and freshly ground
   pepper to taste

pinch of sugar
8 tbsp. olive oil
2 tbsp. tarragon wine vinegar
1 egg yolk

Mix green beans and potatoes with the dressing and let stand for an hour or so. Line a salad bowl with the crisped lettuce leaves, place the marinated vegetables in the center and the tunafish around them. Pour any remaining dressing over them. Then arrange the tomato wedges and egg wedges around the center, cover egg wedges with anchovy filets, scatter olives and pimento and sprinkle with parsley.

Served with crisp French bread and a glass of chilled wine, a salade Niçoise is the perfect luncheon dish for warm weather.

French Potato Salad
(for 4)

6 medium potatoes (the waxy
   kind, like russets)
salt and pepper to taste
$\frac{1}{3}$ cup olive oil
3 tbsp. vinegar
4 tbsp. hot water
   (or chicken stock)

1 tsp. Dijon mustard
2 tbsp. grated onion
2 tbsp. parsley, chopped
2 tsp. capers, squeezed
   dry and chopped

Boil potatoes until cooked but still somewhat firm. Peel and slice thin. Sprinkle with oil, vinegar, season with salt and pepper, turn carefully with a wooden spoon and fork. Mix mustard with hot water, add, along with onion, capers, and parsley, to potatoes. Blend carefully once more and let stand for an hour or two. Do not refrigerate; this potato salad should be served at room temperature.

Marinated Mushrooms
(for 4)

2 cups very small firm mushrooms

3 cups water

1 tbsp. shallots, minced

1 small onion, sliced

1 small clove garlic, minced

2 tbsp. lemon juice

2 tbsp. olive oil

1 tsp. Dijon mustard

1 tsp. shallots, very finely minced

1 tbsp. parsley, minced

cooking oil

salt and pepper

Add shallots, onion, garlic, lemon juice, salt, pepper and olive oil to the water, bring to a boil, add mushrooms and simmer, covered, for about 6 or 7 minutes. Remove mushrooms with a slotted spoon, cool them and put them in a serving dish. Blend $1/3$ cup of the cooking liquid with the mustard, shallots and parsley, add a little lemon juice if needed, also some oil, and correct seasoning with salt and pepper. Pour over the mushrooms and cool.

Braised Endive Vinaigrette

(for 4)

4 medium endives
½ cup water
½ tbsp. lemon juice
1 tbsp. oil

1 tsp. sugar
salt and white pepper
1 tbsp. parsley, minced
vinaigrette sauce *(p. 12)*

Trim root end of endives, remove any loose leaves, wash and put in a casserole. Add water, lemon juice, oil, sugar, salt and pepper. Bring to a boil, cover and simmer for about 45 minutes. Remove endives, let cool and squeeze out most of the cooking liquid. Shape them, put in a serving dish, cover with vinaigrette, sprinkle with parsley.

Leeks Vinaigrette
(for 4)

6 medium sized leeks
vinaigrette sauce *(p. 12)*
1 tsp. Dijon mustard
1 tbsp. parsley, minced

1 tsp. chives, chopped
1 tsp. shallots, very finely
  minced

Trim leeks, use the white part only. Cut them lengthwise in half and wash carefully under running water. They are usually quite sandy. Simmer them in salt water for about 45 minutes until tender. Remove, drain well and cool. Mix vinaigrette with mustard, add herbs and shallots, blend and cover leeks with the sauce. Let stand for an hour before serving.

Anchoiade
(for 4)

2 cloves garlic
1 small can anchovies
1 tbsp. olive oil
1 tsp. vinegar
pepper to taste

1 tbsp. tomato paste
5 black olives, chopped
  fine
4 slices firm white bread

Pound garlic in a mortar, add the anchovies and the oil from the can, continue pounding until a coarse paste is formed. Blend in the olive oil, tomato paste, vinegar and pepper. Toast bread (under the broiler) on one side only. Spread the anchovy mixture on the hot un-toasted side of the bread, press the mixture down firmly and cook in 475° oven for 4 minutes.

La Pipérade
(for 4)

5 tbsp. ham fat
1 small onion, minced
1 clove garlic, minced
1 large sweet red or green
   pepper, cored, seeded and
   coarsely chopped
2 tomatoes, peeled, seeded
   and chopped

pinch of cayenne pepper
pinch of basil
salt and pepper to taste
5 eggs
4 slices smoked ham or
   prosciutto
1 tbsp. butter

Heat ham fat in skillet. When rendered add onion and saute until it turns light golden, add pepper and saute 3 more minutes. Add tomatoes, garlic, cayenne pepper, basil, salt and pepper and simmer until the tomatoes are very soft, crush and stir with a fork. Add the well-beaten eggs and cook very gently until they begin to thicken, stirring a couple of times.

In the meantime fry the ham slices in butter and pour the fat from the fried ham over the eggs. Put eggs on a hot serving platter, top with the ham slices and garnish with toast triangles.

Grand-Mère Chanarts Crêpes au Gratin

(for 4)

1 recipe crêpes *(p. 145)*
3 cups sauce béchamel
  (p. 7)
2 egg yolks
¼ cup crème fraîche
  (p. 20) or heavy cream
¼ tsp. grated nutmeg

pinch of cayenne pepper
¼ lb. cooked ham, sliced
¼ lb. Gruyère cheese,
  sliced
1 cup grated Gruyère
¼ cup butter, melted

Prepare the crêpe batter and fry 12 large crêpes, about 8 inches in diameter. Keep them warm.

Make the béchamel. Beat together the egg yolks and the crème fraîche and mix into the béchamel, beating virorously. Season with nutmeg and cayenne. Cut the ham and Gruyère into thin julienne strips and add about three quarters of them to the béchamel. Spoon a little of this sauce on each crêpe and roll it up. Place the crêpes side by side in a buttered baking dish and spoon the remaining béchamel over them. Sprinkle with grated cheese and melted butter and top with the remaining strips of ham and cheese. Bake in preheated 400° oven for about 10 minutes.

Beer Fondue
(for 2)

1⅓ cups beer
¼ lb. Swiss swiss, or Gruyère
cheese, diced very small
1 tbsp. tomato puree

pinch of cayenne pepper
1 tsp. kirsch
1 tsp. cornstarch
French bread, cut into
bite-size cubes

Put beer in saucepan and bring to a boil. Reduce by two-thirds. Add the cheese, tomato puree and cayenne pepper. Cook over lowest possible heat, stirring constantly, until cheese has melted and the fondue has thickened and is smooth. Blend the kirsch and the cornstarch and then stir it into the fondue. Cook for another half minute, while stirring. Eat in the usual way by dipping the bread cubes into the fondue.

Croque-Monsieur
(for 4)

8 slices of firm white
bread
4 slices smoked ham
½ cup butter, softened

4 slices of Swiss cheese
¼ cup Swiss cheese,
grated

Trim the crusts off the bread slices and butter them. The slices of ham and cheese should be trimmed to the same size as the bread. Put ham and cheese on 4 of the bread slices, top with the remaining bread. Put these sandwiches in a buttered baking dish, sprinkle with grated cheese and bake in a preheated 400° oven for 15 minutes.

Mushrooms Côte d'Argent
(for 6)

12 firm white mushroom caps,
    medium to large size
lemon juice
2 dozen large, pimento-
    stuffed olives
3 cloves garlic, minced

2 anchovy filets, minced
1 tbsp. olive oil
¼ lb. cooked ham, ground
white breadcrumbs
salt and pepper to taste
butter

Remove mushroom stems, wipe the caps gently with a damp cloth. Add lemon juice to 3 cups of water, bring to a boil and blanch the mushrooms for 2 minutes. Drain well. Combine all other ingredients except butter. Fill each mushroom cap heaping full, dot with a small piece of butter and bake in a preheated 425° oven for 10 minutes.

Croutes au Fromages
(for 2)

1 tbsp. peanut oil
3 thin slices of smoked
  bacon, diced
2 ounces cream cheese
  (½ small package)

¼ lb. Swiss cheese, diced
  small
pinch of cayenne pepper
4 slices of firm white
  bread, toasted

Heat the oil in a saucepan, add the bacon and let it cook gently until transparent but not crisp. Add the cream cheese, Swiss cheese and cayenne pepper. Cook over low heat, stirring constantly with a wooden spoon until the mixture is smooth and thick. Put the toast in a shallow, lightly buttered baking dish, spread cheese mixture on top and put under the broiler until top is browned and bubbly.

Ham Soufflé

(for 4)

3 tbsp. butter
3 tbsp. flour
1 cup plus 2 tbsp. milk
salt to taste
pinch of cayenne pepper
4 eggs, separated

pinch of grated nutmeg
1 cup grated Gruyère
 cheese
½ cup smoked ham,
 finely diced

Melt the butter in a saucepan, add the flour and stir over low heat until the mixture is light golden. Stir in 1 cup of the milk. Stir constantly and bring to the boiling point, season with salt, cayenne and nutmeg. Remove from heat and cool slightly. Beat together the egg yolks and the remaining milk and stir them into the white sauce. Correct seasoning and stir in ham and grated cheese. Beat the egg whites until stiff and fold them into the mixture. Butter and flour a 1½ quart soufflé dish and pour in the mixture. Bake in a preheated 375° oven for about 30 minutes. Serve immediately.

Leek Tart
(for 4)

1 recipe pâté brisée
   (p. 143)
3 large leeks
3 tbsp. butter
1 cup crème fraîche
   (p. 20) or heavy
   cream

1 cup milk
4 eggs
salt to taste
freshly ground white pepper
pinch of grated nutmeg
¼ cup fine dry bread-

Prepare the pâte brisée, roll it out to ⅛ inch thickness and with it line a 9-inch pie plate or flan ring placed on a baking sheet. Trim off the roots and green part of the leeks, wash them well and cut them into thin slices. Blanch them in boiling salted water for 5 minutes. Drain and rinse under cold running water, drain well again. Heat the butter in a heavy saucepan and gently sauté leeks in it until they are soft. Do not let them brown.

Beat together the crème fraîche, milk and the eggs, season with about 1 teaspoon of salt, pepper and nutmeg. Spread the leeks on the tart, cover with egg mixture and sprinkle with breadcrumbs. Bake in preheated 350⁰ oven for about 30 minutes or until a knife inserted into the custard comes out clean. Serve immediately.

Onion Tart

(for 4)

1 recipe pâté brisée
  (p. 143)
4 large onions
3 tbsp. butter
1 cup crème fraîche
  (p. 20) or heavy
  cream

1 cup milk
4 eggs
1 cup grated Swiss
  cheese
salt and white pepper
½ cup fine white bread-
  crumbs

Make the paté brisée and let rest for an hour. Cook onions in butter in a heavy saucepan over low heat for about 10 minutes or until they are soft. Do not let them brown. Beat the crème fraîche together with the milk, eggs, and grated cheese. Season to taste with salt and pepper. Roll out the pastry to ⅛ inch thick, line with the pastry a 9-inch pie plate or a flan ring placed on a baking sheet. Spread the onions on the pastry and pour egg mixture over the onions. Sprinkle with breadcrumbs. Bake in preheated 350⁰ oven for about 30 minutes. Serve immediately.

Pissaladière Niçoise
(for 4)

Bread dough (enough to
  make a 12-inch circle)
3 tbsp. olive oil
2 tbsp. butter
1 lb. onions, sliced very
  thin
2 cloves garlic, minced

12 anchovy filets, drained
3 ripe tomatoes, peeled,
  seeded and quartered
16 small pitted black
  olives
salt to taste

Roll dough into a circle, 12 inches in diameter, the edges thicker than the center. Place the dough on well oiled baking sheet. Spread with onions, sprinkle with garlic, then arrange tomato quarters, anchovies and olives and season with salt. Bake in a preheated 400° oven for about 25 minutes or until the outside edges of the dough are slightly browned.

Stuffed Breast of Veal Niçoise — See page 105 for recipe.→

Eggs Meurette
(for 4)

½ cup butter
½ lb. bacon, cut into
   narrow strips
1 medium onion, chopped
1 clove garlic, minced
2 whole cloves
2 cups dry red wine
½ cup chicken broth
½ tsp. sugar

salt and pepper to taste
bouquet garni (parsley),
   thyme, bay leaf)
4 slices of firm white
   bread, crusts trimmed off
8 eggs
2 tbsp. beurre mainé
   (p. 16)

Heat 3 tablespoons of the butter in a casserole, add the bacon, onion and garlic. Sauté until they are golden. Add cloves, wine, broth and sugar, salt and pepper and the bouquet garni. Simmer covered for about half an hour.

Fry the bread slices on both sides in the remaining butter until they are golden and keep warm on a hot serving dish.

Strain the sauce into a skillet, reserve the bacon strips. Bring the sauce to the boiling point and poach the eggs in it, pushing the whites gently over the yolks with a spatula. Remove eggs with a slotted spoon, drain and place two on each slice of fried bread. Quickly thicken the sauce with the beurre manié, pour over eggs and top with the bacon strips.

←*Eggs Meurette.*

Eggs and Mushrooms à la Crème

(for 4)

6 very large,
  firm mushrooms
lemon juice
2 tbsp. butter
1½ tbsp. shallots, minced
1 clove garlic, minced
2 tsp. tarragon

1 tbsp. chives, finely
  chopped
salt and pepper to taste
6 eggs
½ cup crème fraîche
  (p. 20) or heavy
  cream

Take stems off mushrooms and discard. Wipe caps with damp cloth and moisten slightly with lemon juice to prevent discoloring. Butter a shallow baking dish, spread shallots and garlic and place mushrooms, stem side down in the dish. Saute for a few minutes over medium flame. Then turn the caps over. Season each with salt, pepper, a sprinkle of tarragon and chives and place in each a tiny pat of butter. Then cook them in a preheated 400° oven for 3 to 4 minutes, basting once. Remove from oven. Break one egg into each cap, season with a little salt and pepper, cover with crème fraîche. Cover the dish and return to oven for 3 minutes or so, until the eggs are done to your taste.

Codfish à la Portugaise

(for 4)

2 tbsp. butter
2 tbsp. olive oil
2 tbsp. onion, minced
1 large clove garlic,
   crushed
1 cup canned tomatoes,
   drained
¾ cup dry white wine
1 carrot, peeled and chopped

1 small bay leaf
1 pinch dried thyme
1 tbsp. parsley, chopped
1 pinch dried marjoram
cayenne pepper to taste
salt and pepper to taste
4 codfish steaks (about
   2 inches thick)

In a casserole, sauté onion and garlic in butter and oil until light golden. Add all other ingredients except cod steaks, bring to a boil, cover and simmer gently for 15 minutes. Then add fish, cover and simmer for another 15 minutes until fish is flaky. Remove fish carefully to a hot serving platter. Reduce sauce quickly until thickened to the consistency of light cream. Rub through a sieve and pour over the fish.

Note: Cod or haddock filets can be used instead of the steaks. The cooking time, however, will be shorter.

Timbale of Flounder
(for 4)

3 large flounder filets
(about 1¼ lbs.)
1½ tbsp. butter
1 tbsp. flour
⅓ cup hot milk
2 egg yolks, beaten
salt and white pepper to
taste

1 tbsp. dry sherry
½ tsp. paprika
small pinch cayenne pepper
2 egg whites, beaten stiff
1 cup heavy cream,
whipped
parsley

Put fish filets in a food processor with the steel blade or in a blender, and process until puréed. Melt butter in a saucepan, stir in the flour and stir until the mixture is hot and bubbling. Do not let brown. Gradually stir in the hot milk, simmer for 2 minutes, reduce heat to barely simmering and blend in the egg yolks, salt, pepper, sherry, paprika and cayenne. Simmer, but do not let boil, stirring constantly until the mixture thickens, for a minute or two. Remove from heat and blend in the puréed fish. Cool the mixture, then fold in the beaten egg whites and the whipped cream, pour into a greased ring mold. Put the mold in a pan partly filled with hot water, place in a preheated 350⁰ oven and bake for 30 minutes. Unmold on a serving platter, garnish with parsley sprigs and serve with Hollandaise sauce.

Filet of Flounder Amandine

(for 2)

milk or beer
flour
2 flounder filets (about
  ½ lb. each)
2 tbsp. corn oil
3 tbsp. butter
pepper

¼ cup slivered, blanched
  almonds
1 tbsp. lemon juice
2 tbsp. parsley, minced
1 peeled lemon, cut in
  pieces
parsley

    Dip filets first in milk or beer, then coat them with flour. Cook them quickly in oil and butter until golden brown on both sides. Don't over-cook. Transfer filets to a hot serving dish and keep hot. Add almonds and lemon juice to pan juices, cook, stirring constantly until almond slivers are golden brown. Pour almonds and pan juices over filets, sprinkle with parsley, garnish with lemon slices.

Filet of Sole Marguery

(for 2)

1 sole (2 lbs.)
1 cup dry white wine
2 cups water
1 large onion, sliced
1 carrot, sliced
1 sprig parsley
2 tbsp. parsley, minced
½ bay leaf

salt and pepper to taste
2 egg yolks
3 tbsp. butter, cut in
  pieces
18 mussels, scraped, steamed
  and shelled
½ lb. medium shrimp, cooked,
  shelled and deveined

Filet the sole or have it done at the fishmarket. Keep the head, bones, skin and trimmings. Make the fish stock: Combine in a saucepan the fish head, bones, skin and trimmings with the wine, water, onion, carrot, parsley and bay leaf. Simmer for half an hour and then strain through a fine sieve. Put the filets in a buttered baking dish, add the fish stock and season with salt and pepper. Poach over low heat for about 5 minutes. Pour the liquid in which the fish was cooked into a saucepan. Reduce it over high heat to a scant cup. Remove from heat, beat in the egg yolks and swirl in the butter pieces to make a smooth sauce. Add the parsley and coat the filets with this sauce. Glaze them quickly under the broiler, arrange the mussels and shrimp around the filet and serve.

Paupiettes of Sole
or Flounder
(for 6)

1 cup firm mushrooms,
  minced
3 tbsp. butter
$1/3$ cup shallots, chopped
$1/3$ cup parsley, chopped
1 cup chives, chopped
1 small clove garlic
  minced
6 filets of sole or flounder
2 eggs
salt and pepper to taste

$1/2$ cup milk
fritter batter *(p. 14)*
dry white breadcrumbs
5 tbsp. butter
3 tbsp. flour
1 cup dry white wine
1 cup crème fraîche *(p. 20)*
  or heavy cream
pinch of cayenne pepper
$1/4$ cup grated parmesan

Sauté mushrooms in butter for 3 minutes, then add shallots, chives, parsley and garlic, sauté until the shallots are soft. Season filets with salt and pepper, spread some of the mushroom mixture on each, roll them up and fasten with toothpicks. Beat eggs and milk, dip fish rolls in the egg mixture, then roll in breadcrumbs and finally dip in the batter. Let them rest for 15 minutes before cooking.

Melt 5 tablespoons butter in a heavy skillet, brown the fish rolls gently on all sides, then remove carefully and keep warm. Stir flour into the skillet, blend with the butter used in frying, then add the wine. Blend well and let simmer until the sauce is smooth and has thickened. Add the crème fraîche, blend well, heat through. Spoon the sauce over the fish, sprinkle with cheese and put under the broiler until golden brown.

Filet of Sole Veronique
(for 6)

6 sole filets
1 tbsp. butter
2 shallots, finely minced
salt and pepper to taste
½ cup white wine

½ cup fish stock (or water)
1 cup seedless grapes,
    peeled
2 tbsp. butter

Flatten the filets slightly with the flat of a knife, season with salt and pepper and roll them up. Fasten the rolls with toothpicks. Butter a shallow baking dish with one tablespoon butter, sprinkle the shallots on top and then place the filets in the dish. Pour the white wine and stock (or water) in the pan, cover and simmer gently for 10 minutes, until the fish is done. Remove the fish carefully to a heatproof serving dish or casserole, reduce the cooking liquid over high heat to about ½ cup. Remove from fire and swirl in 2 tablespoons butter, small pieces at a time. Arrange grapes around the fish, coat the fish with the sauce and put under a hot broiler for a minute or so.

Mackerel in White Wine
(for 4)

1 lb. mackerel filets
1 onion, thinly sliced
1 carrot, peeled and sliced
  paper thin
1 sprig parsley
half a bay leaf

1 pinch of thyme
1 cup dry white wine
salt and coarsely ground
  pepper
1 tbsp. lemon juice

    Place the filets in a baking dish, season with salt and pepper, cover them with the onion slices and carrots and add the herbs. Add wine and lemon juice, bring to a boil and simmer for 5 minutes. Cover the baking dish and let the fish cool. Then remove filets carefully and put in a serving dish, strain the cooking liquid over them, add the cooked onion rings and garnish with the carrot slices, a few lemon wedges and a sprig of fresh parsley.

Skate à la Crème
(for 4)

2 to 3 lbs. skate wings,
   cut into portion pieces*
fish court bouillon to cover
   (p. 14)
4 tbsp. butter
$^1/_3$ cup crème fraîche *(p. 20)*
   or heavy cream

2 egg yolks
$^1/_4$ cup dry white wine
2 tbsp. parsley, minced
1 pinch mace
small pinch cayenne pepper
salt and pepper to
   taste

Rinse fish, simmer in court bouillon for 15 to 20 minutes. Remove from liquid, slide off the skin and put fish on a hot serving platter. Cover with the following sauce: melt butter in top of a double boiler over simmering, but not boiling water. Add the cream and stir until heated through. Blend in the wine, beat the egg yolks until they are creamy and then add them to the sauce, along with mace, cayenne, salt and pepper. Stir with a whisk until the sauce thickens and is hot. Add parsley and coat the fish with the sauce.

*Most fishmarkets carry skate or can order it for you.

Matelotte Bourgeoise
(Eel Stew)
(for 4)

2 lbs. eel, skinned, cleaned, and cut into 3-inch sections
1 tbsp. butter
1 medium onion, sliced
1 large clove garlic, minced
bouquet garni (thyme, bay leaf, parsley)
salt and pepper to taste
2 cups dry red wine
2½ tbsp. beurre manié *(p. 16)*
8 very small white onions
8 small firm mushrooms
3 tbsp. butter
¼ cup cognac

In a heavy saucepan sauté onion and garlic in butter for 3 or 4 minutes. Then add the eel, bouquet garni, salt and pepper and red wine. Bring to a boil and let simmer for 10 minutes. Add the beurre manié in small pieces, stir gently until they dissolve and continue simmering for about 6 minutes, until the sauce has thickened and is smooth. In the meantime, sauté onions and mushrooms in 3 tablespoons butter until light golden and cooked. Remove bouquet garni from sauce, add onions and mushrooms to the simmering stew, add the brandy and ignite. Stir, correct seasoning and serve.

Whiting à la Bretonne
(for 4)

8 whiting filets
6 tbsp. butter
1½ tbsp. shallots, minced
1 tbsp. parsley, minced
1 tsp. capers, minced

¼ cup dry white wine
1 tsp. Dijon mustard
salt and pepper to taste
½ tsp. lemon juice

Put filets in a well-buttered shallow baking dish. Sprinkle shallots, parsley and capers on the filets, stir mustard into the wine and pour over the fish. Dot with pieces of butter, season with salt and pepper and simmer on top of the stove over gentle heat for about 15 minutes. Then drain off the cooking liquid, reduce it over high heat to about half a cup, add to it 1½ tablespoons of melted butter and the lemon juice. Correct seasoning, coat the filets with the sauce and brown quickly under the broiler.

Pochouse
(Fresh-water Fish Stew)
(for 4)

¾ cup salt pork, blanched
and diced

12 small white onions, par-
boiled for 10 minutes

3 lbs. fish, eel and other,
like pike, bass, pickerel,
cut into thick slices

½ bay leaf

4 large cloves garlic,
crushed

pinch of thyme

dry white wine to cover

2 tbsp. beurre manié
(p. 16)

2 tbsp. parsley, minced

Render diced salt pork until golden, pour off most of the rendered fat, add the onions to the pot. Place the sliced fish on top, then the garlic, bay leaf and thyme, salt and pepper and sufficient white wine to barely cover the fish. Bring to a boil, simmer for about 20 minutes, then add beurre manié and dissolve by shaking the pan. Do not stir — this would break the fish. If the sauce is too thick, add a little more wine. Correct seasoning. Serve garnished with fried bread triangles.

Scallops Bonne Bouche
(for 4)

1 lb. bay scallops
$1/3$ cup dry (white) vermouth
1 clove garlic, crushed
½ cup dry white bread-
    crumbs

6 tbsp. butter
salt and pepper to taste
minced parsley
lemon wedges

Put scallops in a bowl, add vermouth, garlic, salt and pepper, mix and marinate for about 30 minutes. Then drain and blot scallops dry with paper towels. Mix them well with the breadcrumbs. Heat butter in skillet until bubbling, add scallops and sauté quickly, over high heat, until they are browned. This should not take longer than 3 or 4 minutes. Put on hot serving platter, sprinkle with parsley and garnish with lemon wedges.

Note: The breadcrumbs are not used as a breading. They will not adhere to the scallops. They serve to soak up any moisture during cooking and as a contrast in texture to the scallops.

Coquille St. Jacques Provençale

(for 4)

2 medium tomatoes, peeled,
   seeded and chopped
2 cloves garlic, crushed
1 shallot, minced
2 tbsp. parsley, minced
1 tsp. chives, minced

2 tbsp. dry vermouth
1 tbsp. butter
salt and pepper to taste
1 lb. bay scallops
¼ cup flour
4 tbsp. butter

Sauté garlic and shallot for 2 minutes in one tablespoon butter. Do not let brown. Add tomatoes, parsley, chives, salt, pepper and vermouth. Blend and simmer for 10 minutes. Dredge scallops in flour; using another skillet, sauté in 4 tablespoons butter over fairly high heat for about 3 minutes, until scallops have browned. Then add tomato mixture, stir well and simmer 2 more minutes. Serve in scallop shells and spoon the sauce on top.

Lobster à l'Armoricaine
(for 4)

2 live 2-lb. lobsters
3 tbsp. oil
½ cup minced onions
4 shallots, minced
salt and pepper to taste

2 cups tomato sauce
¼ cup brandy
2 tbsp. Madeira
2 tbsp. butter

Put the lobsters into boiling water (or court bouillon) *(p. 14)* and cook for 10 minutes after the water returns to a boil. Drain lobsters and cool slightly. Cut the tails, shells and all, into thick slices, split the upper bodies lengthwise in half; discard the sac behind the head, reserve the tomalley and coral, if any. Sever the claws from the bodies and crack them.

Heat the oil in a casserole and saute onions and shallots until they are soft. Add all of the lobster pieces, season with salt and pepper to taste and saute them for about 5 minutes. Add the tomato sauce, cook for 5 minutes and add the brandy. Simmer over low heat for 15 minutes. Transfer the lobster pieces to a hot dish.

Strain the sauce and return it to the casserole. Stir in the reserved tomalley and the mashed coral. Add the Madeira. Reduce the sauce by about one third and correct the seasoning. Stir in the butter. Return the lobster pieces to the sauce and keep over lowest possible heat until serving time. Serve with plain boiled rice.

Lobster à l'Armoricaine.→
Coq au Vin de Pomerol — See page 77 for recipe.→

Lobster à la Landaise

(for 2)

two 1½ lb. lobsters
4 tbsp. butter
3 tbsp. armagnac brandy
  (or cognac)
1¼ cups crème fraîche
  (p. 20) or heavy cream

pinch of cayenne pepper
pinch of tarragon
½ tsp. Pernod (optional)
salt and pepper to taste
1 egg yolk, beaten

Boil the lobster for 10 minutes in salt water or court bouillon, cool and remove meat from shells. Also remove any coral and the tomalley (liver) and reserve. Slice the lobster tails about ¾ inch thick, cut the claws in half. Melt butter in a casserole, when hot add lobster meat and claws, pour brandy over it and ignite. Then simmer gently for about 5 minutes, add crème fraîche, cayenne, tarragon, salt, pepper and Pernod, the coral and tomalley. Blend well and simmer for another 2 or 3 minutes. Remove some of the sauce, blend with the beaten egg yolk, return mixture to casserole, blend, heat through and serve.

←*Braised Young Turkey* — See page 85 for recipe.
←*Green Peppersteak* — See page 97 for recipe.

Sautéed Oysters
(for 3 or 4)

2 dozen oysters
1½ tbsp. butter
1 tbsp. flour
½ cup dry white wine
1 tbsp. shallots, finely minced

1 small clove garlic, minced
½ cup minced mushrooms
cayenne pepper to taste
salt and pepper to taste

Open oysters, strain their liquor. Cook the oysters in their liquor until edges start to curl. Remove oysters with slotted spoon and reserve oysters and their liquor. Sauté shallots and garlic in butter for a few minutes. Do not let brown. Add mushrooms, cook one minute longer. Stir in the flour, sauté another 2 minutes, stirring often, then add wine and oyster liquor, blend well and simmer for a few minutes until the sauce has thickened. Season with cayenne, salt and pepper, add oysters, bring to boil and serve immediately.

Coq au Vin de Pomerol
(for 6)

2 tbsp. oil
4 tbsp. butter
20 tiny white onions
¼ lb. bacon, cut into
thin strips
1 chicken (4 lbs.)
¼ cup brandy
1 bottle Pomerol or
good Burgundy wine

salt and pepper to taste
1 tbsp. sugar
4 tbsp. flour
2 cloves garlic, mashed
bouquet garni (parsley, tarragon, small bay leaf)
10 mushroom caps
2 tbsp. minced parsley and
chives

Heat half the oil and half the butter in a casserole, sauté the onions until they are about to take on color, add the bacon strips. Blend and cook over low heat until onions are tender and the bacon transparent.

Cut the chicken in eight pieces. Remove onions and bacon with a slotted spoon and reserve. Brown the chicken pieces in the casserole on all sides. Season with salt and pepper, sprinkle with brandy and flame. Heat the wine and sugar in a separate saucepan. Sprinkle the flour over the chicken and then add the hot wine to the casserole, along with the garlic and the bouquet garni. Simmer covered over low heat for about 40 minutes.

Sauté the mushroom caps in the remaining butter and oil in a skillet for about 5 minutes. Reserve them with the onions and bacon.

When the chicken is fully cooked, discard the bouquet garni, add mushrooms, onions and bacon. Heat through, transfer everything to a serving platter, sprinkle with parsley and chives. Garnish the platter with fried slices of bread.

Chicken à l'Estragon
(for 4)

3 lb. roasting chicken
5 tbsp. butter
salt and pepper
1 tsp. tarragon
1 tbsp. cooking oil
2 carrots, peeled and diced

4 shallots, minced
½ cup chicken broth
pinch of grated nutmeg
½ tsp. tarragon
2 tsp. arrowroot, dissolved
in 2 tbsp. chicken broth

Sprinkle salt and pepper in the cavity of the chicken, also the tarragon and one tablespoon of butter. Truss the chicken. Put 2 tablespoons butter and the oil in a heavy casserole, heat and brown the chicken on all sides. Pour off fats and add remaining two tablespoons of butter. Add carrots and shallots and sauté until vegetables are soft but not browned. Put chicken on the vegetables, add the broth, nutmeg and tarragon, cover and cook gently for about 1 hour or until chicken is tender. Put whole chicken on serving platter, or cut it into portions first, add dissolved arrowroot to sauce, simmer for 5 minutes until it thickens, correct seasoning and pour over chicken.

Chicken à la Paloise

(for 4)

2½ lb. chicken
salt and pepper
4 tbsp. olive oil
3 tomatoes, peeled, seeded
   and chopped
4 green peppers, seeded
   and sliced lengthwise
2 cloves garlic, crushed

1 cup firm sliced mush-
   rooms
¼ lb. smoked ham, diced
½ cup dry white wine
3 tbsp. armagnac brandy
   (or cognac)
chopped parsley

Cut chicken into 6 pieces, and season with salt and pepper. Heat olive oil in a heavy casserole and sauté the chicken pieces until golden brown, about 10 minutes. Add tomatoes, peppers, garlic, mushrooms, ham and white wine. Cover and cook gently for about half an hour or until chicken is tender. Remove chicken pieces to hot platter, blend sauce with a whisk and reduce until fairly thick. Return chicken to casserole, pour brandy over it and ignite. Sprinkle with parsley before serving.

Chicken à la Crème

(for 4)

5 tbsp. butter
1 chicken (3 lbs.)
   cut in pieces
1½ tbsp. flour
salt and white pepper
pinch of nutmeg and
   powdered ginger

¾ cup chicken broth
¾ cup dry white wine
1 cup crème fraîche
   (p. 20) or heavy cream
2 egg yolks
1 bouquet garni (parsley,
   tarragon, ½ small bay leaf)

Sauté chicken pieces in butter for about 20 minutes over gentle heat. Turn them occasionally but do not let them brown. Then sprinkle with flour, salt and pepper, turn them a few more times, cover and simmer for 10 minutes. Add the wine, chicken broth, bouquet garni, nutmeg and ginger and simmer covered for 15 minutes or until the chicken is tender. Remove the chicken pieces and keep them hot. Blend cream into the sauce and cook, barely simmering, for 10 minutes. Beat egg yolks with a whisk until they are light colored and creamy, blend a half cup of the cream sauce into them and then add them to the sauce. Blend well, correct seasoning, pour over the chicken and serve.

Chicken Sautéed with Riesling

(for 4)

1 frying chicken, 2½ to 3 lbs. cut in pieces
1 tbsp. cooking oil
4 tbsp. butter
¼ lb. firm mushrooms, sliced
3 tomatoes, peeled, seeded and chopped
1½ cups Riesling or other dry white wine
2 tbsp. brandy
salt to taste
pinch of cayenne pepper
1 clove garlic, minced
3 tbsp. parsley, chopped

Heat oil and butter in casserole. Add chicken and sauté until pieces are browned on all sides. Add mushrooms and tomatoes, cook gently for about 5 minutes. Add the wine and brandy, salt and cayenne pepper. Bring to a boil, cover and simmer for 25 minutes. Remove chicken pieces, put on hot serving dish and keep hot. Skim fat off the pan juices, add parsley and garlic and reduce slightly over high heat. Correct the seasoning and pour sauce over chicken.

Chicken aux Aromates
(for 4)

1 frying chicken, 2½ to 3 lbs., cut in pieces
16 fresh tarragon leaves
8 basil leaves
16 tiny rosemary sprigs
salt and pepper to taste
1 tbsp. cooking oil

20 very small white onions, peeled
12 small, firm mushroom caps
1 clove garlic, minced (opt.)
4 tbsp. butter

Force into the flesh of each piece of chicken or push under the skin 2 tarragon leaves, 1 basil leaf and 2 sprigs of rosemary. (You may use very small amounts of dried herbs, but fresh ones are very much better.) Season the chicken pieces with salt and pepper. Put oil and 2 tablespoons butter in a casserole and sauté the chicken over fairly high heat until golden brown on all sides. Remove the pieces and keep them hot. Add the remaining butter to the casserole, also onions and mushroom caps and garlic, if desired. Simmer for 5 minutes, return chicken to casserole, cover and simmer for about 25 minutes. Put chicken on hot serving dish, skim fat off the sauce, pour the sauce over the chicken and serve.

Chicken à la Marseillaise

(for 4)

1 frying chicken (3 lbs.)
   cut in 8 pieces
2 tbsp. Pernod or Ricard
⅛ tsp. ground Spanish saffron
8 tbsp. olive oil
salt and pepper to taste
2 onions, chopped
4 cloves garlic, mashed
6 tomatoes, peeled, seeded
   and chopped
1 tbsp. parsley, chopped

1 small head fennel, white
   part only, chopped
4 potatoes, peeled and
   thickly sliced
4 slices French bread
For the sauce (Rouille):
1 clove garlic, mashed
4 small hot red peppers
¼ cup olive oil
1 chicken liver
1 tbsp. butter

Reserve the chicken liver. Marinate the chicken in 3 tablespoons of olive oil, Pernod and saffron, salt and pepper for about 30 minutes. Turn the pieces occasionally. Heat 3 tablespoons olive oil in a casserole, add onions and garlic and sauté them just until light golden. Add the tomatoes and cook, stirring occasionally for 5 minutes. Add fennel, parsley, chicken pieces and their marinade, and enough boiling water to just cover the chicken.

Cover and cook over low heat for 10 minutes. Add potatoes, simmer covered for 15 more minutes or until chicken and potatoes are almost cooked. Uncover casserole and continue cooking until the liquid has reduced and slightly thickened. Line a soup tureen or bowl with bread slices, sprinkle the remaining 2 tablespoons of oil over them. Put chicken, vegetables on top and pour sauce over them.

To make the Sauce Rouille: Process garlic cloves, hot peppers and olive oil in a blender. Sauté the chicken liver quickly in butter, mash and add to the mixture. Add 2 slices of potatoes from the stew, also 6 tablespoons of gravy, blend again.

Chicken Breasts Cordon Bleu

(for 4)

4 whole chicken breasts (boned and skinned)

4 thin slices smoked ham

4 thin slices Gruyere cheese

3 tbsp. parsley, minced

4 shallots, minced

1 cup flour, seasoned with salt

2 eggs, beaten with 1 tbsp. oil and 1 tbsp. milk

1 cup fine white dry breadcrumbs

4 tbsp. butter

3 tbsp. cooking oil

lemon wedges

Have butcher flatten the breasts to about ½ inch thickness. Place 1 slice of ham and 1 slice of cheese, the size of half a breast on each half. Fold the other half over it and trim edges neatly. Dredge them first in flour, dip them into the egg, oil and milk mixture, and then roll in breadcrumbs. Flatten them with your hands and let stand for an hour. Heat oil and butter and sauté the breasts about 6 minutes on each side, until golden brown. Garnish serving platter with lemon wedges.

Braised Young Turkey

(for 6)

1 young turkey (5 lbs.)
salt and pepper
4 tbsp. lard
3 carrots, minced
1 small turnip, minced
2 stalks celery, minced
2 onions, minced

1 clove garlic, minced
thin sheets of fresh pork fat
bouquet garni (bay leaf,
    thyme, tarragon)
2 tomatoes, quartered
3 cups chicken broth
3 tbsp. beurre manié (p. 16)

Wipe the turkey inside and out with a damp cloth, season inside and out with salt and pepper. Heat the lard in a casserole and brown the turkey on all sides. Remove and keep warm. Put the carrots, celery, turnip and onions in the casserole, add a little more lard if necessary and cook until the vegetables are soft and golden. Season with salt and pepper, add garlic and mix well. Remove the vegetables from the casserole with a slotted spoon.

Line the bottom and sides of the casserole with the sheets of pork fat and put turkey in the casserole. Add the vegetables, bouquet garni, the tomatoes and the broth. Cover the turkey with another sheet of pork fat.

Cover the casserole, bring the liquid to a boil and then put the casserole in a preheated 350° oven for about 1¾ hours. Remove the turkey, put it on a serving dish and keep hot. Skim the fat off the liquid in the casserole, strain through a fine sieve, let stand for 5 minutes and skim fat off again. Return sauce to low heat, stir in beurre manié. You should use 1 tablespoon of beurre manié for each cup of braising liquid. Simmer for 10 minutes, correct seasoning and serve the sauce separately in a sauceboat. Garnish platter on which turkey is served with watercress.

Duck à la Vasco da Gama

(for 4)

1 duck (5 lbs.)
salt and pepper to taste
$\frac{1}{3}$ cup sugar
$\frac{1}{4}$ cup vinegar
2 cups chicken broth, or
   stock made with duck,
   giblets and back

2 tbsp. cornstarch
   diluted in 2 tbsp. water
2 tbsp. red currant jelly
juice of 1 orange
2 tbsp. curaçao
6 oranges

Season the duck cavity with salt and pepper and truss the bird. Prick the lower breast and thighs with a fork to allow fat to escape. Roast the duck in a preheated 350⁰ oven for 1¼ hours or until the juice runs clear when the thigh is pricked with a fork.

While the duck is roasting make the sauce: In a heavy saucepan make a light caramel by stirring the sugar over low heat until it melts. Add the vinegar and hot chicken broth. Stir and simmer for 3 minutes, then add cornstarch and simmer for 5 minutes. Finally stir in the currant jelly, orange juice and curaçao. Keep hot over low heat.

Prepare the oranges: Peel the zest (skin) from four of the oranges. (There must be no white membrane.) Cut zest into julienne strips, blanch them in boiling water to cover for 3 minutes and drain. Using a very sharp knife cut off the white part from these four oranges, cut out the sections so that they are skinless. Set aside both the orange strips and the sections until the duck is ready. Use the remaining two oranges to make baskets as shown in illustration (p. 17).

When the duck is fully cooked, place it on a hot serving dish, arrange the orange sections around it and put an orange basket at each end. Sprinkle the orange strips over the bird and coat with the sauce.

Salmi of Duck
(for 4)

1 duck (5 lbs.)
8 tbsp. lard
salt and pepper to taste
¼ cup armagnac brandy
¼ cup minced fat from
    Virginia or prosciutto
    ham
20 very small white onions,
    4 of them stuck with
    2 cloves each

6 shallots, minced
4 tbsp. flour
¼ lb. salt pork, blanched and
    finely diced
1 bouquet garni
pinch of nutmeg
4 cups dry red wine
8 slices of French bread
6 tbsp. butter or lard
1 clove of garlic

Cut the duck in serving pieces. Heat the lard in a large, heavy casserole until it is very hot and brown the duck pieces on all sides. Pour all fat off casserole, season the duck pieces with salt and pepper, sprinkle them with armagnac and flame.

Remove the duck pieces and the pan juices from casserole and reserve. Add the ham fat to the casserole and sauté until the fat is rendered. Then add the shallots and white onions and cook over gentle heat until the onions are golden brown. Sprinkle with flour and stir well, then add the diced salt pork, nutmeg and the bouquet garni. Stir in the wine and bring to a boil. Add the duck pieces and their pan juice, correct seasoning and simmer over low heat for an hour or until duck is tender. Fry the bread slices in butter or lard until golden, then rub on both sides with the garlic clove. Remove duck to hot serving platter, strain the sauce through a fine sieve, reduce quickly by about $1/3$ of the volume, then pour over duck. Garnish the dish with the fried bread slices.

Duck à la Normande
(for 4)

1 duck (about 5 lbs.)
salt and pepper to taste
1 cup Muscadet wine
¼ cup calvados brandy
   or applejack

1½ cups crème fraîche
   (p. 20) or heavy cream
6 tbsp. butter
4 apples, peeled, cored
   and quartered

Wipe the cavity of the duck with a damp cloth, season it with salt and pepper and truss the bird. Prick the lower breast and thighs with a sharp fork. Roast in preheated 350⁰ oven for 1¼ hours or until the juices run clear when thigh is pricked with a fork. Remove the duck to hot plate and keep warm. Pour off all the fat from the roasting pan and add the Muscadet to the pan. Stir to deglaze pan and cook until the wine has nearly evaporated. Lower the heat a bit, add the calvados and the crème fraîche, bring to the simmering point and cook until the sauce is thick and smooth. Stir frequently. Remove it from heat and stir in 2 tablespoons of butter. Keep hot but do not reheat the sauce. Quickly sauté apple pieces in the remaining butter in a skillet until golden. Carve the duck, put it in a deep serving dish and coat with the sauce. Garnish with the apple slices.

Casserole of Squab and Peas
(for 4)

5 tbsp. butter
4 squabs
1/3 cup diced smoked bacon
12 small white onions
1 heart of Boston or bibb
   lettuce, shredded
1½ tbsp. beurre
   manié (p. 16)

¾ cup chicken broth
1 tbsp. meat extract
   (Bovril or similar)
2 cups shelled peas
12 small mushroom caps
pinch of tarragon
3 sprigs of parsley
salt and pepper to taste

Truss the squab, heat butter in a heavy casserole and sauté squab on all sides for about 10 minutes, until nicely browned. Pour off about half of the butter, add bacon, onions and lettuce and simmer for 15 minutes. Add all other ingredients except beurre manié, cover and cook gently for about half an hour or until squab are tender. Remove squab, cut in half and keep hot. Stir beurre manié into the gravy, let simmer for a few minutes until thickened, return squab and heat through.

Note: "Squab" chicken, weighing about 1 or 1¼ pound, or small fresh Cornish hens can be used instead of squab.

Tournedos Chasseur
(for 4)

4 slices beef filet, about
   ¼ lb. each
6 tbsp. butter
3 tbsp. cooking oil
4 shallots, minced
¼ lb. firm mushrooms, minced
1 cup dry white wine

¾ cup beef broth
1 tsp. beef extract (Bovril
   or other)
1 tbsp. tomato paste
1½ tbsp. beurre manié *(p. 16)*
salt and pepper
2 tbsp. minced parsley

    Heat half the butter and all the oil in a casserole and sauté the tournedos over high heat quickly until well browned on both sides and done to taste. Remove to a serving dish and keep hot. Add remaining butter to the pan juices, together with the shallots and mushrooms. Sauté for about 5 minutes or until golden. Add the wine, bring to a boil and reduce quickly by two thirds. Then add the beef broth, beef extract and tomato paste. Stir in the beurre manié. Simmer sauce for 5 more minutes. Season with salt and pepper. Return tournedos to casserole and turn them in the sauce to coat them, but do not let them cook any further. Return them to serving dish, coat with the sauce and sprinkle with parsley.

Pork Chops Charcutière — See page 117 for recipe.➙

Boeuf Bourguignon

(for 4)

3 tbsp. cooking oil

2 lbs. beef (chuck, sirloin, or "chicken steak") cut in 1½ inch cubes

1 tbsp. flour

3 cloves garlic, minced

3 cups red Burgundy wine

1 cup water

1 bouquet garni (thyme, bay leaf, parsley)

salt and pepper to taste

pinch of grated nutmeg

½ lb. lean salt pork, rinsed and diced

24 small white onions, peeled

Heat oil in heavy saucepan, brown the meat cubes over high heat. Then drain off oil, dust with flour, blend with spoon and sauté until flour is browned, being careful not to burn it. Then add wine, water, garlic, bouquet garni, salt and pepper. Cover and simmer for about 1½ to 2 hours or until meat is tender. You can also cook it in a 350° oven. Sauté the salt pork cubes in a skillet until lightly browned, then add peeled onions and sauté, stirring occasionally until onions are also lightly browned. Skim fat off the simmering stew, remove the bouquet garni, drain the fat off the skillet and add onions and pork bits to the stew. Heat through, skim fat off again, correct seasoning and serve. Small peeled carrots, cooked separately, also sautéed mushroom caps can be added just before serving.

←*Ragout of Pigs' Trotters* — See page 121 for recipe.

Fondue Bourguignonne
(for 6)

3 lbs. sirloin steak
2 cups cooking oil
salt and pepper

a variety of sauces hot and
cold (Béarnaise, mustard,
remoulade, Bordelaise, etc.)

Trim the meat carefully, cut it in cubes of about 1½ inches. Skewer a few on a long wooden skewer. Place oil in fondue or other bowl over an alcohol lamp and heat oil. Let each guest dip his skewer into the hot oil and cook the meat to individual taste. Put sauces in individual bowls to be used according to taste.

Carbonnade à la Flamande
(for 6)

2 large onions, sliced thin
6 tbsp. butter
6 steaks, 1 inch thick,
   about 1 lb. each
½ cup cooking oil
1 large clove garlic,
   chopped
salt and pepper to taste
pinch of thyme
1 small bay leaf

pinch of nutmeg
1 tbsp. tomato paste
4 tbsp. brandy
3 cups dark beer (or 1½
   cups stout and 1½
   cups beer)
1½ cups beef stock
1 tbsp. beurre manié
   (p. 16)

Melt butter in a deep saucepan. Sauté onion slices until golden brown, about 15 minutes, stirring occasionally. In a heavy skillet brown the steaks in hot oil on both sides. Then put the steaks on top of the onion into the saucepan. Add garlic, bay leaf, thyme and nutmeg, pour the brandy over it and flambé. Then add salt and pepper, beer, beef stock and tomato paste, bring to a boil, cover and bake in a preheated 375° oven for about 1½ hours or until steaks are soft. Remove steaks to hot platter. Remove bay leaf from sauce. Stir in beurre manié and reduce over hot fire until sauce has thickened. Pour sauce over steaks and serve.

Boeuf Braisé

(for 8)

4 to 5 lbs. bottom round
  or blade chuck
3 tbsp. flour
2 tbsp. butter
1 Bermuda onion, thinly
  sliced
1 large clove garlic, minced

1 tbsp. lemon juice
1 pinch thyme
1 cup dry red wine
salt and pepper to taste
2 tbsp. beurre manié *(p. 16)*
3 tbsp. cognac (opt.)
1½ cups canned tomatoes

    Heat butter in a heavy saucepan or kettle. Sprinkle meat with flour and brown on all sides in butter. Add onion, garlic, tomatoes, lemon juice, thyme and red wine. Stir, season with salt and pepper. Cover and cook over gentle heat for about 3 hours or until meat is done. Remove meat to hot platter, add beurre manié to sauce and stir until dissolved and the sauce has thickened. Add the cognac, flame, coat the meat with the sauce and serve the rest in a sauceboat.

Green Peppersteak
(for 1)

1 well-trimmed sirloin or
   porterhouse steak, about
   about ¾ lb.
salt to taste
1 tbsp. green peppercorns
   coarsely crushed

2 tbsp. oil
2 tbsp. butter
¼ cup armagnac brandy
   or cognac
½ cup crème fraîche
   (p. 20) or heavy cream

Season the steak with salt and rub in the green peppercorns. Heat oil and butter in a deep skillet, sauté the steak on both sides until done to taste. Transfer it to a hot serving dish and keep warm. Pour off the pan juices, add the brandy to the skillet and scrape off all the brown bits on the bottom of the skillet. Heat and ignite the brandy. Stir in the crème fraîche, bring to a simmering point and reduce by half. Do not let it boil fast or the sauce might curdle. Coat the steak with the sauce and serve.

Note: Green peppercorns are available in most markets in jars or cans, packed either in vinegar or water. Drain before crushing.

Steak Tartare
(for 1)

1/3 lb. finely ground or
    chopped lean steak
    or filet
2 egg yolks
pepper and salt to taste
1 tsp. Dijon mustard
1 tbsp. olive oil

1 tsp. lemon juice
pinch of cayenne pepper
1/4 cup minced onion
1/4 cup capers, drained
1/4 cup minced parsley
1/2 tsp. Worcestershire sauce
1 tbsp. ketchup (opt.)

Put the ground steak in a bowl and season with salt and pepper. Blend in gently one egg yolk, the mustard, oil, lemon juice, cayenne, 2 tablespoons of minced onion, 1 tablespoon of the capers, 1 tablespoon of the parsley, Worcestershire sauce and ketchup.

Shape the steak into a mound and put it on a serving plate. Press an empty eggshell half into it, filled with the other egg yolk, and surround it with the remaining capers, onions and parsley.

Let each diner blend the eggyolk into the steak and add, if so desired, more onion, capers and parsley.

Serve with thinly sliced dark bread. A cup of hot consomme goes especially well with steak tartare.

Shoulder of Lamb Landaise
(for 4)

1 shoulder of lamb, boned
  (about 3 lbs.)
¼ lb. veal, ground
¼ lb. lean pork, ground
¼ lb. chicken livers, minced
1 cup fresh white bread-
  crumbs
2 tbsp. parsley, minced

1 tbsp. brandy (opt.)
salt and pepper to taste
3 tbsp. oil
3 tbsp. butter
4 firm tomatoes, cored
3 cups cooked, buttered
  leaf spinach

Have butcher bone the shoulder, and trim off any fat. Blend the veal, pork and livers (or ask your butcher to grind them together), add breadcrumbs, parsley and brandy, salt and pepper and mix well. Spread the shoulder of lamb flat, place filling in the center and roll up. Tie securely with kitchen string. Heat oil and butter on top of the stove and brown the rolled lamb on all sides. Roast in a 400⁰ oven for about 1 hour. Baste frequently and turn several times to cook evenly on all sides. When meat is three-quarters done, place tomatoes in the pan, baste them and finish cooking.

Before serving, remove string, put the meat on a hot serving platter and spoon the pan juices over the meat. Surround the meat with mounds of hot buttered spinach and top each mound with a tomato.

Leg of Lamb Boulangère

(for 5 or 6)

1 leg of lamb, about 5 lbs.
2 tbsp. oil
2 tsp. paprika
1 tbsp. Dijon mustard
1 tbsp. lemon juice
2 large cloves garlic,
   crushed to a paste

1 tsp. rosemary, crushed
¼ tsp. thyme
2 lbs. potatoes
1 large Bermuda onion,
   sliced thin
butter
about 2 cups beef broth
salt and pepper to taste

Trim most fat off the leg of lamb. Blend oil, paprika, mustard, lemon juice, garlic, rosemary and thyme. Rub this paste into the lamb and let stand for a couple of hours. Peel the potatoes and boil them in salt water until barely done. Sauté onion slices in butter until they start to turn golden. Slice the potatoes, about ¼ inch thick, put a layer in the bottom of a roasting pan, cover with a layer of sauteed onions and put another layer of potatoes on top. Spoon the beef broth over it, add salt and pepper. Place the leg of lamb on top of the potatoes and roast in a 350⁰ oven for about 17 minutes a pound for pink lamb or longer, according to taste. Baste a few times with the pan juices.

Stuffed Leg of Lamb
(for 6)

1 leg of lamb (about 5 lbs.)
¼ lb. ground veal
¼ lb. ground lean pork
6 chicken livers, chopped
1 cup fresh white breadcrumbs
salt and pepper to taste
pinch of cayenne pepper

pinch of dried thyme
1 tsp. crushed dried rosemary
   leaves
2 tbsp. parsley, minced
1 clove garlic, minced
3 carrots, peeled and chopped
1 medium onion, chopped

Bone and butterfly the leg of lamb or have your butcher do it. Trim off most of the fat. Make the stuffing: mix veal, pork, chicken livers, breadcrumbs, parsley, cayenne, salt and pepper. Lay the boned leg of lamb flat. Sprinkle the surface with thyme and rosemary, spread the filling over the meat, roll it up and tie it in a neat roll or fasten it securely with skewers. Spread carrots, onion and garlic in the bottom of a baking dish or small roasting pan, add a little water and cook in a preheated 375⁰ oven for about one hour or according to taste.

Navarin of Lamb Printanier

(for 4 to 6)

2 lbs. lean lamb
1 tbsp. flour
1 tbsp. cooking oil
1 tbsp. butter
1 bouquet garni (parsley, stalk of celery, thyme and ½ bay leaf, tied together
1 cup chicken broth
1 tomato, peeled, seeded and chopped
2 cloves garlic, minced

1 tbsp. butter
8 small white onions, peeled
2 white turnips, peeled and quartered
3 small carrots, peeled and cut in half lengthwise
½ cup frenched string beans
½ cup green peas
8 new small potatoes
salt and pepper to taste

Cube the meat, sprinkle with flour and sauté in oil and butter until browned. Pour off fat, and add chicken broth to pan. Bring to a boil, stirring to prevent scorching and to deglaze the pan. Season with salt and pepper. Add tomato, bouquet garni and garlic. Cover the pan and simmer gently. In another pan sauté onions and turnips until golden brown. Add to the stew along with the carrots, beans and potatoes. Simmer covered for 30 minutes, then add peas and continue simmering for another 15 minutes or until meat is done. Discard bouquet and skim off excess fat before serving.

Lamb Chops Champvallon

(for 2)

4 tbsp. cooking oil

4 tbsp. butter

3 tomatoes, peeled, seeded and chopped

3 potatoes, peeled and thinly sliced

½ tsp. dried thyme

1 bay leaf

salt and pepper to taste

2 large lamb chops, trimmed

2 onions, minced

1 clove garlic, minced

Heat half the oil and half the butter in a casserole, add the tomatoes and cook until they are soft. Then add the potatoes, thyme, bay leaf and garlic. Add salt and pepper to taste and just enough hot water to cover the potatoes. Cover and simmer over low heat for about 20 minutes. When the potatoes are done they should have absorbed all the water. If not, uncover and boil the water away.

Put remaining oil and butter in a skillet, season chops and brown them quickly on both sides. Add onions and continue cooking until onions are golden brown and the chops are done to your taste. Then place chops on top of the potatoes, spread onions on top and pour pan juices from skillet over the chops. Cover the casserole and simmer for another 2 minutes.

Lamb Kidneys in Mustard Sauce

(for 4)

8 lamb kidneys
3 tbsp. butter
1 small clove garlic,
   minced
1 cup firm mushrooms,
   sliced
1½ tbsp. Dijon mustard
1 tbsp. beef extract (Bovril
   or similar)

¾ cup chicken broth
½ cup dry white wine
½ tbsp. beurre manié *(p. 16)*
2 tsp. capers,
   drained and chopped
½ bay leaf
salt and coarsely ground
   pepper to taste

Skin the kidneys, split them in half and cut out the fatty core. Brown them quickly in butter, remove from pan and keep warm. Add mushrooms and garlic to pan, sauté for 3 minutes, stir in mustard and cook for another minute. Add broth, meat extract and wine, stir well and then add the beurre manié. Let mixture come to simmer and stir until beurre manié has dissolved and sauce starts to thicken. Add capers, bay leaf, salt and pepper, return kidneys to pan, cover and simmer 10 minutes.

Stuffed Breast of Veal Niçoise

(for 6)

1 breast of veal

6 tbsp. olive oil

½ cup raw rice

2 cups fresh white bread-
crumbs

lukewarm milk

¼ lb. salt pork, finely
diced and blanched

½ cup chicken livers

¼ lb. grated Swiss cheese

½ lb. spinach, blanched and
finely chopped

2 egg yolks

¼ tsp. dried basil

salt and pepper to taste

pinch of grated nutmeg

1 large onion, chopped

2 medium carrots, chopped

1 leek, white and green
part, washed and chopped

Ask your butcher to bone the breast and cut a pouch for stuffing. Ask
for the bones.

Heat 1 tablespoon oil in a casserole, add the rice, stir and sauté a
couple of minutes until the rice becomes translucent. Add ¾ cups water
and a little salt, bring to a boil, cover and simmer for 15 minutes or until
rice is tender.

Soak the breadcrumbs in lukewarm milk, squeeze them dry. Mince
salt pork and chicken livers, mix them with the cooked rice, breadcrumbs, spinach, grated cheese, egg yolks and basil. Season with salt,
pepper and nutmeg. Stuff the breast of veal with this mixture and sew
the opening together.

Put the chopped vegetables into a heavy casserole with the remaining oil and the veal bones. Spread them over the bottom of the casserole;
put the veal breast on top and cook over high heat for 7 minutes. Turn
the breast and cook again for 7 minutes. Cover the casserole and cook in
350⁰ oven for 2½ hours. After 1 hour of cooking pierce the meat with a
needle in 3 places. Turn meat occasionally and baste. Drain the cooked
meat. Put it in a serving dish. Skim fat off pan juices and strain the
juices over the meat. Chill well and serve cold, garnished with sliced
tomatoes and black olives.

Blanquette of Veal
(for 4)

2 lbs. veal from shoulder
  or breast, cut into 1½
  inch pieces
3 medium carrots, sliced
12 small white onions,
  peeled
1 clove garlic, chopped
1 stalk celery
3 sprigs parsley
1 bay leaf
salt and pepper to taste

2 cups chicken broth
  (or water)
2 tbsp. shallots, minced
3 tbsp. butter
12 small firm mushrooms
3 tbsp. flour
2 egg yolks
⅓ cup crème fraîche *(p. 20)*
  or heavy cream
minced parsley

    Put meat, carrots, onions and garlic in a casserole. Tie celery, parsley and bay leaf together and add to the meat, season with salt and pepper and add chicken broth. Let it come to a boil, turn heat low and simmer for a few minutes. Take scum off the surface, cover the casserole and simmer for an hour or more, until meat is done. Sauté shallots in a skillet in 2 tablespoons butter until soft but do not let brown. Add mushrooms and sauté until they take on color. Remove mushrooms and add them to the casserole. Add remaining butter to the skillet, stir in the flour and cook the roux, stirring for a couple of minutes. Then add gradually ¾ cup sauce from the casserole to the roux, stir constantly until smooth. Blend egg yolks and crème fraîche and add, while whisking, to the skillet. Heat through but do not let boil. Stir this sauce into the casserole, let it thicken for a few minutes. Stir in lemon juice, correct seasoning. Remove the tied celery and parsley, sprinkle blanquette with parsley before serving.

Veal Marengo
(for 4)

2 lbs. shoulder of veal or
   boneless veal shank
1½ tbsp. olive oil
1½ tbsp. butter
1 medium onion, chopped
3 tomatoes, peeled, seeded
   and chopped
12 small firm mushrooms

2 tbsp. flour
½ cup dry white wine
1 cup chicken stock
1 clove garlic, minced
salt and pepper to taste
3 tbsp. cognac
minced parsley

Cut the veal in fairly large cubes, heat oil and butter, add veal, onion and tomato. Sauté over medium heat for 15 minutes, stirring occasionally. Then add mushrooms. Continue cooking until most of the liquid has evaporated. Stir in flour, add wine, chicken stock and garlic, season with salt and pepper, stir well. Cover and simmer for about one hour or until meat is tender. Uncover, reduce sauce if too thin, add cognac and flame. Sprinkle with parsley before serving.

Veal Birds Brumaire

(for 4)

For the stuffing:

$^1/_3$ lb. ground veal

$^1/_3$ lb. lean pork, ground

$^1/_3$ lb. smoked ham or
    prosciutto, ground

8 slices of veal, about
    $^1/_4$ inch thick, cut from
    the upper leg

salt and pepper to taste

flour

3 tbsp. oil

1 tbsp. butter

1 tbsp. lemon juice

1 cup Madeira wine

1 tbsp. cornstarch blended
    with 2 tbsp. water

    Combine the stuffing ingredients. Flatten the veal cutlets (or ask your butcher to do it) with the flat side of a cleaver. Season them with salt and pepper, put a little of the stuffing on each. Roll them up and tie them securely with kitchen string. Dust the veal birds with flour, and sauté them in the combined oil and butter over high heat until they are golden on all sides. Turn them frequently. Reduce the heat, cover and simmer them for 15 minutes.

    Transfer veal birds to a hot serving dish and keep hot. Stir the Madeira and the lemon juice into the pan juices, boil for a few minutes, stir to deglaze, then add the cornstarch mixture. Cook stirring until the sauce has thickened. Correct the seasoning, skim fat off the sauce. Coat the veal birds with the sauce and serve.

Veal Birds Brumaire.→

Veal Cutlets à la Russe

(for 4)

4 loin veal chops, cut ¼
   inch thick
softened butter, the weight
   of the boned chops
fresh white breadcrumbs
   soaked in milk, squeezed
   dry, also the weight of
   the boned chops

salt and pepper to taste
pinch of grated nutmeg
flour
6 tbsp. butter
1 lemon, sliced

Bone and trim the chops, reserve the bones. Grind the meat (or have your butcher do it), using the finest blade of the grinder. Weigh the meat and then beat into the ground meat the same weight of softened butter and of fresh white breadcrumbs soaked in milk and squeezed dry. Season with salt, pepper and nutmeg.

Divide the mixture into four pieces and form them in the shape of the original chops around the bones. Dust lightly with flour and sautè in hot butter in a skillet until golden brown on both sides.

Place on a serving dish and garnish with lemon slices.

←*Veal Cutlets à la Russe.*

Veal Chops Sauce Piquante
(for 4)

4 veal chops
3 tbsp. butter
2 tbsp. wine vinegar
4 tbsp. heavy cream
2 tbsp. water
2 tbsp. olive oil

1½ tsp. Dijon mustard
1½ tsp. capers,
   drained and chopped
1 anchovy filet, chopped
salt and pepper to taste

Sauté chops in butter over gentle heat for about 6 minutes on each side until browned and done. In another pan blend all other ingredients, heat for a few minutes just to the simmering point but do not let boil. Remove chops from pan, pour off any fat and add the cream mixture to the pan, simmering and scraping gently to deglaze the brown pan juices. Return chops to pan, heat through without letting the sauce boil.

Braised Veal Shank

(for 2)

2 tbsp. cooking oil
2 tbsp. butter
1 veal (hind) shank, cut
  in half
1 onion stuck with 1 clove
2 carrots, chopped
1 turnip, chopped
1 heart of celery (white
  part) chopped
2 slices bacon, minced
salt and pepper to taste

3 tomatoes, peeled, seeded
  and chopped
  bouquet garni (rosemary,
  parsley, small bay leaf)
1½ cups dry white wine
peel of a small lemon, yellow
  only, cut into thin slivers
8 small new potatoes
juice of a small lemon
2 tbsp. parsley, minced

    Heat oil and butter in a heavy casserole. Sauté meat until browned on all sides. Add onion, carrots, turnip, celery and bacon, cover and simmer for about 10 minutes. Then add tomatoes, wine, bouquet garni, lemon slivers, salt and pepper. Cover casserole and simmer for about one hour. Peel the potatoes, add them to the casserole, add a little more liquid if necessary and simmer for another 25 minutes. Then remove the meat and put it on a hot serving platter, surrounded by the potatoes. Keep hot. Strain pan juices through a fine sieve, skim off fat, put back into casserole and add lemon juice. Reduce quickly if sauce is too thin. Correct seasoning and pour over the meat.

Veal Cutlets à la Crème
(for 4)

4 veal cutlets pounded thin
(about ¼ lb. each)
2 tbsp. lemon juice
white salt and pepper to taste
2 tbsp. butter
4 tbsp. dry (white) vermouth

½ cup crème fraîche
(p. 20) or
heavy cream
½ tsp. tarragon
finely minced parsley

Sprinkle the cutlets with lemon juice, season with salt and pepper and sauté them in butter for 3 minutes on each side. Then add the vermouth, cook for another minute. Reduce the heat and stir in the crème fraîche, parsley and the tarragon. Simmer for 5 minutes, stirring once in a while. Correct seasoning and serve.

Calf Liver Pâté Lyonnaise
(for 10)

4 cups fresh white bread-
  crumbs
lukewarm milk
3 medium onions
1 clove garlic
2 lbs. calf liver (pork
  liver may be used instead)
$1/3$ lb. fresh pork fat
salt and pepper to taste
6 eggs

pinch of thyme
pinch of mace
2 tbsp. butter
2 tbsp. lard
thin slices of fresh pork
  fatback
2 carrots sliced
1 cup strong chicken
  broth
¼ cup Madeira wine

Soak breadcrumbs in milk and squeeze them dry. Grind coarsely the onions, garlic, liver and pork fat. Put in a bowl, together with the bread-crumbs, thyme, mace, salt and pepper. The mixture should be quite well seasoned. Add the eggs, butter and lard and blend well. Line a baking dish with the slices of pork fatback, which should be long enough to hang well over the sides of the dish. Spoon in the liver mixture and fold the fat strips securely over the mixture, encasing it completely. Shape it into the form of a roll. Sprinkle sliced carrots on top and bake in a preheated 350° oven for 1½ hours, basting frequently with the chicken broth. About 5 minutes before removing the paté from the oven, baste with Madeira.

This paté can be served hot or cold.

Veal Kidneys Reynière

(for 4)

4 veal kidneys
3 tbsp. butter
2 shallots, minced
½ clove garlic, minced
½ cup firm mushrooms,
  sliced

4 tbsp. calvados (or applejack)
salt and pepper to taste
1 tbsp. parsley, minced
1 tsp. Dijon mustard
¾ cup crème fraîche *(p. 20)*
  or heavy cream

Trim kidneys, remove fat core, and slice them. Sauté shallots and garlic in butter for about 2 minutes, until soft but not browned. Add the kidney slices and the mushrooms and sauté quickly for 5 minutes, until kidney has browned. Add calvados, ignite and when the flame has died down, stir in parsley, season with salt and pepper. Stir in the mustard and the créme fraîche, blend, heat through and serve.

Pork Chops Charcutière

(for 4)

4 tbsp. lard

4 loin pork chops, cut ¾ inch thick and trimmed

salt and pepper to taste

2 tablespoons vinegar

½ cup dry white wine

bouquet garni (bay leaf, thyme and parsley)

1 shallot, minced

1 tbsp. tomato paste

½ cup beef broth

½ tsp. Kitchen Bouquet

1 tsp. beef extract (Bovril or other)

1 tsp. sugar

½ tsp. Dijon mustard

¼ cup thinly sliced sour pickles or cornichons

Heat the lard in a skillet over medium heat. Season the chops with salt and pepper and sauté them in hot lard until they are thoroughly done and golden brown on both sides. Remove the chops, put them on a hot serving dish and keep them hot.

Pour off the fat from the skillet, add the vinegar and boil until the vinegar has almost evaporated. Scrape the pan to deglaze while boiling the vinegar. Add the wine, bouquet garni, shallot, tomato paste, Kitchen Bouquet, beef broth and Bovril, simmer until reduced by one quarter. Remove the bouquet garni, stir in mustard, sugar and pickles, correct the seasoning. Blend well and coat the chops with this sauce.

Pork Chops Gitane
(for 4)

8 pork chops, about ½ inch thick
1 tbsp. butter
1 cup firm mushrooms, sliced
²/₃ cup tomato sauce (canned can be used)
¹/₃ cup cooked ham, julienne cut (in strips)

2 tbsp. white onion, chopped
¹/₃ cup cooked smoked tongue, julienne cut
1 tbsp. parsley, minced
1 small clove garlic, crushed
4 tbsp. dry sherry
salt and pepper to taste

Trim most fat off the chops. Melt butter in a casserole and brown chops on both sides, cover and cook over medium heat until almost done — about 15 minutes. Then add mushrooms, onion and garlic, cover again and cook for 10 more minutes, until meat is soft. Add all other ingredients, simmer for 5 more minutes.

Pork Chops Honfleur

(for 4)

4 thick pork chops, trimmed
1 tbsp. cooking oil
1 tbsp. butter
1½ tbsp. flour
1 cup apple cider
1 tbsp. shallots, minced
1 clove garlic, crushed

1 sprig rosemary (or 1
   tsp. dried)
salt and pepper to taste
1 apple, pared, cored and
   sliced into eighths
2 tsp. lemon juice

In a heavy skillet brown chops in butter and oil, about 5 minutes on each side. Remove chops and keep hot. Pour most of the fat off, add the flour and stir for a minute or two to make a light brown roux. Add cider, shallots, garlic and rosemary, stir well, season with salt and pepper. Simmer sauce for a few minutes until smooth and thickened. Then return chops to skillet, cover and simmer for 15 minutes. Surround with sliced apples, add lemon juice and simmer 10 minutes longer.

Beckenoff
(for 6)

1 lb. boned pork shoulder
1 lb. boned lamb shoulder
1 lb. beef chuck
4 medium white onions, sliced
2 leeks, white part only, sliced
1 tbsp. meat extract (Bovril or similar)

3 cloves garlic, minced
pinch of allspice
bouquet garni (parsley, bay leaf, thyme)
4 cups dry white wine (Riesling type)
2 lbs. potatoes, sliced ¼ inch thick
salt and pepper to taste

Cut the meats in large cubes. Put in a bowl with onions, leeks and garlic. Mix. Add salt, pepper, allspice and bouquet garni. Cover with wine and marinate in the refrigerator for 24 hours. Put half the potatoes in the bottom of a heavy casserole, also half the onions from the marinade. Put meats on top, cover with the rest of the potatoes and onions. Remove bouquet garni and pour remainder of marinade along with the remaining vegetables into the casserole. Stir in the meat extract. Cover and cook in the oven for about 3 hours at 350°. Then skim off any fat from the surface, ladle off most of the liquid and reduce it quickly over hot fire by about one third. Pour it back over the meat and serve.

Ragout of Pig's Trotters

(for 4)

4 pig's trotters (feet)
  cut lengthwise in half
large onion, stuck with
  4 cloves
salt and pepper to taste
4 tbsp. butter
4 tbsp. flour

½ bottle dry white wine
2 cloves garlic, minced
4 carrots, peeled and sliced
1 lb. fresh broad beans or
  lima beans
¼ tsp. allspice

Put pig's trotters in a saucepan, cover with water, add the onion, salt and pepper. Cover and simmer for about 3 hours. Let the trotters cool in the water, then drain and bone them. Reserve the cooking liquid.

Heat the butter in a casserole and stir in the flour. Blend well, then add 2 cups of the cooking liquid and the wine. Stir over medium heat until it comes to a boil, then add the boned trotters, garlic, carrots and beans. Season with allspice. The sauce will be quite thin in the beginning but will thicken during cooking time. Simmer for 45 minutes, then correct seasoning.

Serve with mashed potatoes.

Tripe à la Mode de Caen

(for 8)

¼ lb. salt pork, cut into thin slices

5 lbs. fresh honeycomb tripe

2 calves feet, split in half

3 medium carrots, peeled and halved

2 medium Spanish onions, stuck with 2 cloves each

2 cloves garlic

pinch of nutmeg

pinch of allspice

pinch of rosemary, thyme, small bay leaf, tied in cheesecloth

2 stalks celery and 3 leeks, white part only and halved lengthwise, tied together

6 cups dry white wine

3 cups chicken broth

salt and white pepper

¼ cup calvados brandy or applejack

Wash tripe well and soak, together with the calves feet, in cold water for 3 or 4 hours, changing the water occasionally. Drain and dry. Line the bottom of a heavy, deep saucepan with a tight-fitting lid with the salt pork slices. Cut the tripe in 2 inch long strips and place on top of salt pork, also the calves feet. Add carrots, onions, garlic, herbs, celery, leeks, nutmeg, allspice, salt and pepper. Then cover with wine and chicken broth. Bring to a boil on top of the stove, cover and seal the edges of the pot with aluminum foil or dough. Put in 325⁰ oven and cook for about 8 hours. Then remove tripe, put it in an earthenware serving casserole. Take the meat off the calves feet and cut it in pieces. Add it to the tripe. Strain all the liquid through a fine sieve. Discard all the vegetables. Reduce liquid on top of the stove to about 4 cups. Skim off all the fat and add the calvados. Correct the seasoning and pour it over the tripe. Then simmer for half an hour before serving.

Cooking it the day before and reheating before serving improves the flavor.

Choucroute Garnie Alsacienne
(for 6)

3 lbs. sauerkraut
2 medium onions
3 tbsp. lard
1 cup dry white wine
  (Riesling preferred)
1 apple, peeled, cored,
  and diced
2 cups beef stock
2 dozen juniper berries,
  crushed and tied in
  cheesecloth

1 lb. piece of smoked pork
  belly or lean bacon
1½ lbs. smoked pork loin
1 large garlic sausage
  (Saucisse à l'ail, Polish
  or Italian types)
6 frankfurters
2 tbsp. kirsch brandy
pepper to taste

Heat lard in a heavy casserole, add onion and fry until light golden brown. Wash sauerkraut lightly, squeeze out much of the liquid, add to the onions, stir well and continue cooking for 5 minutes, stirring frequently with a long fork. Mix in the diced apple, add the wine, stock and the juniper berries. The liquids should almost cover the sauerkraut. Cover and simmer for 2 hours. Stir a few times with the fork. Then add the smoked pork belly, cover it with sauerkraut and continue cooking for another 1½ hours. Add a bit more wine and stock if needed. About half an hour before serving stir in kirsch, place the smoked pork loin, frankfurters and sausages on top, cover again and finish cooking. Serve with boiled potatoes.

Carrots Vichy
(for 4)

1½ lbs. carrots
2 tbsp. sugar
3 tbsp. butter
½ cup chicken stock

½ cup dry white wine
salt and white pepper
to taste
2 tbsp. parsley, minced

Scrape or peel carrots and cut in even pieces if they are large. Cook them in wine and chicken stock until almost done. Add sugar, butter, salt and pepper and simmer uncovered until liquid has nearly evaporated and the carrots are done and glazed with a coat of butter. Shake the casserole frequently while cooking. Sprinkle with parsley just before serving.

Cauliflower au Gratin
(for 4)

1 medium head cauliflower
1½ cups Mornay sauce
   (p. 6)
grated Parmesan cheese

fine dry white
   breadcrumbs
butter

   Separate the cauliflower into flowerets and discard core. Wash and cook in salt water until done but still firm. Cover the bottom of an oven-proof baking dish with half of the Mornay sauce, arrange the well drained flowerets on top and cover with the remaining Mornay. Sprinkle with grated cheese, breadcrumbs and top with a few small pats of butter. Cook in preheated 450⁰ oven until top is browned.

Cauliflower in Cream
(for 4)

1 large head of cauliflower
cup crème fraîche
  (p. 20) or
heavy cream

salt and pepper to taste
pinch of grated nutmeg
2 tbsp. butter, cut in small
  small pieces

Blanch the whole cauliflower. Cut the flowerets off the main stem. In a large pot bring water to a boil, season it with salt. Drop the flowerets into the boiling water and cook for about 10 minutes until a knife will easily pierce the stems. Drain well. Pour the crème fraîche in a saucepan and bring to simmering point. Season lightly with nutmeg, salt and pepper and reduce it by half. Put the cauliflower in a hot serving dish, dot with butter, coat with the cream and serve.

Flageolet Beans à la Bretonne

(for 6)

¾ cup dry flageolet beans
3 tbsp. butter
2 tbsp. chopped onions
1 large clove garlic, minced
1 large tomato, peeled, seeded
    and chopped

1 tbsp. tomato paste
1 tbsp. meat extract
    (Bovril or similar)
salt and pepper to taste
1 tbsp. parsley, minced

Soak the beans overnight; they should swell up to make about 4 cups. Cook them in boiling salt water until done but not too soft. Put butter in a saucepan, sauté onions gently until soft, but do not brown, then add garlic, cook for another 2 minutes. Add tomatoes and simmer for 10 minutes. Then blend in tomato paste, meat extract, salt and pepper. Bring to a simmer, stir and mix in the flageolets. Stir gently and simmer for 5 more minutes. Before serving sprinkle with chopped parsley.

Stuffed Eggplant Provençale

(for 4)

4 eggplants
6 large tomatoes, peeled,
  seeded and chopped
3 tbsp. olive oil
salt and pepper to taste
pinch of grated nutmeg
2 tbsp. parsley, minced

1 small bouquet garni
  (thyme, rosemary, oregano,
  basil)
2 cloves garlic, minced
½ cup grated Swiss cheese
4 tbsp. butter, cut in pieces

Cut eggplants lengthwise in half, but do not peel them. Cut several slashes in the cut side of each half, sprinkle with salt and let them stand for 30 minutes. Brush off the salt, scoop out the insides of the halves but leave the shell intact. Mince the scooped-out eggplant.

Sauté the chopped tomatoes in hot olive oil. Season with salt, pepper and nutmeg, add the bouquet garni (tied in cheesecloth), and cook the mixture until the sauce is smooth and thick. Strain the sauce. Mix the sauce with the minced eggplant, add garlic and parsley. Stuff the eggplant shells with this mixture and put them side by side in a buttered baking dish. Sprinkle with grated cheese, dot with butter and bake in a preheated 375° oven for about 30 minutes.

Eggplant Porquerolles

(for 4)

four 1½ inch thick slices
   of eggplant (cut across the
   eggplant)
salt and pepper
⅓ cup olive oil
3 tbsp. butter
2 medium onions, chopped
3 cloves garlic, chopped
¾ cup grated Gruyère cheese

4 tomatoes, peeled, seeded
   and chopped
½ tsp. dried thyme
½ bay leaf, crumbled
½ tsp. oregano
½ tsp. basil
1 tsp. celery salt
½ cup soft white bread-
   crumbs

Put the eggplant slices in an oiled baking dish and sprinkle lightly with salt and pepper. Then pour the olive oil over the eggplant. Broil for about 6 to 7 minutes, then remove and keep warm. Melt butter in a skillet, add onions and cook gently for 5 minutes, then add garlic, tomatoes, stir and simmer for 10 more minutes. Add all the herbs and celery salt, pepper to taste, stir and simmer 2 more minutes. Blend in the breadcrumbs and spread this mixture over the eggplant slices. Sprinkle with the grated cheese and broil for a couple of minutes until browned.

Braised Belgian Endives

(for 4)

4 medium to large endives
1 cup chicken broth
2 tbsp. lemon juice
3 tbsp. butter
pinch of mace

2 tsp. sugar
salt and white pepper to
taste
5 tbsp. butter
2 tbsp. parsley, minced

Blanch the endives in boiling water for 3 minutes. Then drain and gently squeeze out water. Put with all other ingredients, except the 5 tablespoons butter and parsley, in a casserole. Cover and cook in a preheated 350⁰ oven for 45 minutes. Keep hot. Just before serving remove from casserole. Let them drip dry or squeeze gently; melt butter in skillet and when hot add endives. Sauté, turning occasionally until they brown lightly on all sides. Sprinkle with parsley before serving.

Endives au Gratin

(for 4)

8 medium-sized endives
2 cups chicken broth (or water)
2 tbsp. lemon juice
4 thin slices prosciutto ham
(or lean smoked bacon)

1 tbsp. butter
1½ cups Bechamel sauce *(p. 7)*
white pepper and salt to
taste
½ cup grated Parmesan cheese

Trim the root end of the endives, wash and discard loose leaves. Bring broth or water to a boil, add lemon juice and endives and poach gently for about 20 minutes. Drain well, squeeze gently to shape them and place in a buttered baking dish. Cover with prosciutto ham. Spread the bechamel over the endives, sprinkle with salt and pepper and top with grated cheese. Bake in preheated 375⁰ oven for about 15 minutes, until top is light golden.

Braised Lettuce

(for 4)

4 heads Boston or Bibb
  lettuce
4 very thin slices of salt pork
1 thinly sliced onion
1 large carrot, thinly sliced

3 cups beef broth
1 tbsp. meat extract
  (Bovril or similar)
2 sprigs parsley
pepper to taste

    Trim off outer lettuce leaves, wash well and blanch heads in boiling water for 5 minutes. Remove, drain and wash under cold running water. Squeeze gently to remove water, shape the heads neatly and wrap a slice of salt pork around each head. Put onions and carrot in a heavy saucepan, place lettuce on top, add parsley, pepper, beef broth and meat extract. Bring to a boil, cover and cook in a preheated 350⁰ oven for 1 hour. Remove the lettuce, squeeze into uniform shapes. Reduce sauce very quickly and spoon some of it over the lettuce. Finish with a pat of butter on each.

    The hearts of romaine are also excellent when braised. After blanching, fold each in half and then proceed as above.

Braised New Onions
(for 4)

12 new white onions
   (regular medium white
   onions can be used)
2 tbsp. oil
2 tbsp. sugar

½ cup dry red or white
   wine
water
salt and pepper to taste

Put oil in a heavy saucepan just large enough to hold the onions in one layer. Pare onions, and place them in the pan. Start over medium heat and cook until the oil sizzles. Then add wine, sugar, salt and pepper and enough water to cover bottom of the pan 1 inch deep. Cover and cook over medium heat. Add a little more water as needed. Turn the onions occasionally with a spoon, cook for about 2 hours until the liquid in the pan is syrupy and brown. Spoon the liquid over the onions when serving.

Tomatoes Provençale
(for 4)

4 ripe, firm tomatoes
salt and pepper to taste
1 tbsp. parsley, chopped

1 large clove garlic, crushed
¾ cup dry white breadcrumbs
6 tbsp. olive oil

Halve the tomatoes, squeeze out gently the seeds and most of the water. Season the halves with salt and pepper. Mix parsley, garlic and breadcrumbs and spread some on the tomato halves. Then sprinkle them with olive oil. Arrange on baking dish and bake in 450° oven for about 10 minutes until browned or finish browning them under the broiler.

Green Peas à la Française
(for 4)

3 tbsp. butter
⅓ cup lean salt pork,
   blanched and diced
1 heart of Romaine lettuce,
   washed and shredded
12 very small white onions

¾ cup chicken broth
2 cups green peas
1 tsp. sugar
small pinch of thyme
2 sprigs of parsley
salt and pepper to taste

Heat butter in a saucepan, add the diced salt pork and sauté, stirring often, for 10 minutes. Add the shredded lettuce and sauté 5 minutes longer. Then add all other ingredients, cover pan and simmer for 6 minutes. Uncover, and cook until the liquid has evaporated and the onions and peas are cooked. Shake the pan occasionally.

Potatoes Boulangère
(for 6)

3 Bermuda onions,
   sliced thin
2 tbsp. cooking oil
3 tbsp. butter

2 lbs. potatoes
beef broth, about 3 cups
salt and pepper

Peel and cook the potatoes until they are about half done. Drain and slice about ¼ inch thick. Sauté onion slices in oil and butter until limp and starting to turn color. Butter a baking dish. Make alternate layers of potatoes and onions, starting and ending with a layer of potatoes. Salt and pepper, add enough beef stock to barely cover, dot with a few more pieces of butter and bake in 350⁰ oven for about 45 minutes or until all the liquid has evaporated and the top layer has browned.

Crêpes Flambées au Grand Marnier — See page 144 for recipe.→

Potatoes au Gratin
(for 6)

2 lbs. waxy potatoes
2½ cups milk
½ cup light cream
1 large egg
salt and pepper to taste
pinch of mace

¾ cup Gruyère cheese, grated
¼ cup Parmesan, grated
1 clove of garlic
3 tbsp. butter

Peel the raw potatoes, grate them on the coarse side of a vegetable grater (or use a mechanical shredder or food processor) into a pan filled with cold water. Drain potatoes. Fill the pan again with water, wash the potatoes well and drain again. Simmer them in milk for about 5 minutes, taking care not to scorch the milk. Drain and reserve the milk. Beat the egg until light and creamy, add salt, pepper, mace and half of the mixed grated cheeses. Slowly add milk and cream and whisk until well blended. Mix in the potatoes. Rub the inside of a shallow baking dish with the garlic, butter it well and fill with potato mixture. Even the surface, sprinkle with remaining cheese and dot with butter. Bake in preheated 400⁰ oven for 25 minutes until golden brown.

←*Charlotte à la Valentin* — See page 157 for recipe.

Potatoes Gratin Dauphinois
(for 4)

4 Idaho potatoes
   (about 1 ½ lbs.)
salt and pepper
1 clove garlic
1 tsp. thyme

1 cup milk
¼ cup crème fraîche
   (p. 20) or heavy cream
2 eggs

Peel the potatoes and grate them. Season with salt and pepper. Rub the bottom of an earthenware baking dish with the garlic clove. Butter the baking dish. Put the potatoes in the dish in several layers and sprinkle each layer with a little thyme. Blend the milk, crème fraîche and the eggs. Pour over potatoes and lift them gently with a fork or spatula to make sure that the mixture is well distributed. Cook in preheated 350⁰ oven for 30 minutes.

Stuffed Potatoes Niçoise

(for 4)

4 baking potatoes
2 hard-cooked egg yolks
   mashed
2 tbsp. tomato purée
4 anchovy filets, mashed
8 green pitted olives,
   minced

2 tbsp. tunafish in oil, mashed
2 tbsp. olive oil
1 tbsp. each of fresh
   parsley, chives, tarragon,
   basil, minced
salt and pepper to taste

Bake the potatoes in a 375⁰ oven for about 45 minutes or until tender. Cut a slice lengthwise from the top of each potato and scoop out the pulp, taking care not to break the skins. Mash the pulp. Combine the cooked egg yolks, tomato purée, anchovy filets, olives and tunafish, blend with potato pulp, season with salt and pepper. Fill the potato shells, place them side by side in a buttered baking dish and sprinkle with olive oil. Bake in preheated 375⁰ oven for 15 minutes. Before serving sprinkle with the minced herbs.

Parmesan Potatoes au Gratin
(for 4-6)

4 cups boiled potatoes
5 tbsp. butter
½ cup light cream

½ cup grated Parmesan
1 tbsp. butter
2 tbsp. Parmesan

Mash potatoes while still hot with butter and cream and beat until fluffy, adding a little more cream if needed. Blend in Parmesan, season with salt and pepper and put in buttered gratin dish. Dot with a few pats of butter, sprinkle with Parmesan and bake in 375° oven until top is nicely browned.

Mushrooms à la Lyonnaise
(for 4 to 5)

1 lb. firm mushrooms, sliced
3 tbsp. butter
1 tsp. lemon juice
1 clove garlic, chopped
1 tbsp. onion, minced

1 large tomato, peeled, seeded and chopped
1 tbsp. parsley, chopped
salt and pepper to taste

Heat butter, add sliced mushrooms, lemon juice, garlic and onion. Mix and sauté for a minute, then add tomato, and cook until liquid has evaporated. Stir in parsley, season with salt and pepper and serve.

Ratatouille Niçoise

(for 4)

3 zucchini
4 tomatoes
1 small eggplant
2 medium onions
1 head of fennel
  (finocchio)
3 artichoke hearts (fresh
  or canned)
2 green peppers

1 clove garlic, minced
3 tbsp. cooking oil
3 tbsp. olive oil
salt and pepper to taste
pinch of grated nutmeg
2 sprigs of thyme,
  chopped
1 tbsp. lemon juice

Peel the zucchini, tomatoes, eggplant and onion and cut them into thick slices. Trim the fennel and slice it. Remove cap from peppers, also seeds and membranes and slice. Cut the artichoke hearts into small pieces.

Heat the oils in a deep skillet or casserole. Add all vegetables, mix them well and season with salt and pepper, nutmeg, sprinkle with thyme and lemon juice, cover the casserole and simmer very gently for about 30 minutes until the vegetables are soft. Serve hot or cold.

Zucchini à la Provençale
(for 4)

2 lbs. small zucchini

6 tbsp. olive oil

1 medium white onion, minced

salt and pepper to taste

2 large cloves garlic, minced

2 tomatoes, peeled and quartered

1 pepper, seeded and diced

1 small pinch rosemary leaves, crushed

½ tsp. basil

½ cup grated Parmesan cheese

2 tbsp. parsley, chopped

Blanch zucchini by pouring boiling water over them. Cut them lengthwise in half inch thick slices. Put 2 tablespoons oil in a casserole and sauté onion until it turns light golden. Lay tomato quarters on top, season with salt and pepper, add garlic and spread green pepper over tomatoes. Add rosemary and basil. Cover the casserole and cook gently for about 10 minutes. Then arrange the zucchini slices on top, sprinkle with remaining oil, cover again and simmer for 3 minutes or so. Don't overcook the zucchini. Remove cover, sprinkle with cheese and parsley and put for half a minute under the broiler.

Pâte Brisée

(sufficient for one 9-inch tart or about eight 3-inch tartlets)

2 cups sifted all-purpose flour	½ tsp. salt
1 whole egg	3 tbsp. heavy cream
1 extra egg white (for tartlets)	¾ cup sweet butter

Place the flour in large bowl and make a well in the center. Put the whole egg, the salt, cream and butter into it. Gradually blend the flour into the other ingredients. Knead the pastry until smooth. Chill in the refrigerator for at least 2 hours before rolling out.

Tartlet shells generally require more handling than large tart shells and should be made firmer by substituting water for heavy cream and by adding one additional egg white to the other ingredients.

Baking directions:

Roll out the pastry between two sheets of wax paper to a thickness of slightly less than ¼ inch. It should be slightly larger than the flan ring or the tart pan you are using. Remove the top layer of the wax paper; invert the pastry over the tart pan or the flan ring placed on a baking sheet, and peel off the other sheet of wax paper. With the fingers firm the pastry into the pan, leaving it slightly thicker at the top edge. Trim off the excess pastry neatly and make a decorative edge with the blunt end of a knife or your fingers. It is best to freeze the pastry before baking, or at least chill thoroughly. Then fill with any desired filling and bake on the lowest rack in a preheated 375⁰ oven. Fruit tarts should be baked for 1 hour to 1 hour 15 minutes, custard fillings 25 to 30 minutes.

Crêpes Flambées au Grand Marnier
(for 6)

1 recipe crêpes *(p. 145)*

¼ cup sugar

¾ cups of Grand Marnier

Make about 24 **crêpes**. Sprinkle them with sugar, fold them in quarters and put them in a chafing dish. Sprinkle them generously with Grand Marnier, heat the crepes and flame.

Note: You may add the grated rind of 1 or 2 oranges to the crêpe batter to accentuate the orange flavor.

Sautéed Apples Normande
(for 4)

4 large, firm apples

3 tbsp. sweet butter

¼ cup sugar

½ tsp. nutmeg

1 tsp. lemon juice

4 tbsp. calvados (applejack)

Slice the peeled and cored apples neatly in ½ inch thick slices. Melt butter in skillet, add apples and sprinkle with sugar, lemon juice and nutmeg. Cook them gently until they are light golden, then turn very carefully and sauté the other side. When done, pour the Calvados over the apples, ignite and serve.

Basic Crêpe Recipe

(for about 24 crèpes)

1½ cups milk
1 tsp. salt
2 tbsp. sugar
½ cup butter
2½ cups sifted all-
    purpose flour

1 tbsp. vegetable oil
4 eggs
½ cup flat beer

Heat the milk, sugar, salt and butter together in a saucepan until the butter has completely melted. Put the flour in a large bowl and make a well in the center. Pour the oil into the well and add the eggs. Mix thoroughly, beating with a wire whisk. Add the milk mixture and then stir in the beer. Strain the batter through a fine sieve and let it rest in the refrigerator for 2 hours before using it.

To fry the crêpe use a heavy iron skillet with sloping sides or a French crêpe pan. These pans come in various sizes and should be used only for making crêpes. Grease the pan very lightly with butter or oil, heat the pan over fairly high heat until the fat is nearly smoking, pour about two tablespoons of batter into the pan, just enough to cover the bottom, and fry for about one minute or until browned. Turn with a spatula, or, with enough dexterity, give the pan a sharp rap and toss the crêpe to turn it. Fry for about 30 seconds on the other side. Crêpes can be cooked well in advance and stacked one on top of the other.

Diplomat Pudding

(for 6-8)

1 recipe Vanilla Bavarian
   Cream *(p. 154)*
25 to 30 plain ladyfingers
½ cup kirsch brandy
1 cup mixed raisins and
   dried currants

¾ cup mixed glacéed
   fruits
2 tbsp. thick apricot
   preserve
2 cups fruit sauce (apricot,
   raspberry or strawberry)

Make a Bavarian cream but do not allow it to set. Soak the lady-fingers in kirsch and plump the raisins and currants in lukewarm water. Oil the bottom of a 10-cup mold and then rinse the mold in cold water. Arrange the glacéed fruits in the bottom of the mold and then fill the mold with alternate layers of Bavarian, ladyfingers, raisins and currants and apricot preserve, ending with a layer of ladyfingers. Chill for several hours before serving. Serve it with a fruit sauce.

Rice à l'Imperatrice
(for 6)

¾ cup long grain rice
(do not use processed
rice)
5 cups milk
2-inch piece vanilla bean
²/₃ cups candied fruit
and candied peels, chopped
¹/₃ cup kirsch brandy
1 cup fine sugar

2 envelopes unflavored
gelatin
1 tbsp. water
3 eggs separated
2 cups heavy cream,
whipped
1 cup raspberry sauce or
other brandied fruit sauce

Marinate candied fruit in kirsch. Put rice, 4 cups milk and the vanilla bean in a heavy pan and cook very slowly over gentle heat until all the milk is absorbed. Do not cover the pan. When the milk has been absorbed add a little more, stir with a fork and continue to cook and add milk until the rice is creamy and mushy. Beat egg yolks and sugar until creamy. Moisten gelatin in cold water, then dissolve in a little hot water and add to egg yolks. Put the cooked rice in a mixing bowl, let cool slightly. Put the bowl in a larger one filled with crushed ice. Stir in the egg yolk mixture. Stir until rice is quite cool. Beat the egg whites and fold into the rice, then the candied fruit with their liquid, fold in the whipped cream. Oil a mold very lightly, rinse with cold water and fill with the rice. Chill for several hours before unmolding. Spoon a little of the raspberry sauce over the rice and serve the rest in a sauceboat.

Clafoutis
(for 6)

3 cups dark sweet ripe
   cherries
½ cup sugar
2 egg yolks
1 whole egg

½ cup butter, softened
1 cup flour
2 tbsp. rum
¼ tsp. almond extract
1 cup milk

Beat together the sugar and egg yolks and when they are well blended, beat in the whole egg. Gradually add the butter, beat again, and stir in the flour. Then beat more energetically. Stir in the rum, the almond extract and finally the milk. The batter must be very smooth. Pit the cherries without tearing them apart. Put them in a heavily buttered 8 to 9 inch baking dish. Pour the batter over the cherries. Bake immediately on a lower rack of a preheated 400° oven for about 40 minutes.

Crème Brulée
(for 4)

2 cups heavy cream
1 tbsp. cognac (opt.)
½ pinch piece vanilla bean

4 large egg yolks
1 cup granulated sugar

Put the cream in a small saucepan, add the vanilla bean and bring to a simmer and remove from heat. Beat the egg yolks with 5 tablespoons sugar and cognac until light and creamy. Blend cream, spoon by spoon, into the beaten eggs, put the mixture in a heavy pan and heat gently until it coats a spoon. Then pour it into a shallow Pyrex dish, and refrigerate the custard overnight. Before cooking, spread sugar over the entire surface of the custard, set the dish in a larger one, filled with crushed ice and put it under a hot broiler to caramelize the sugar. (Watch constantly since the top can burn very rapidly.) Once the top is a uniform layer of caramel, remove from broiler, cool and refrigerate for 5 minutes.

Peach Cup Foyot
(for 4)

4 ripe firm peaches
lemon juice
1½ cups raspberries*
3 tbsp. kirsch brandy

½ cups heavy cream
1 tablespoon sugar
a few drops vanilla
   extract

Dip peaches for a minute in boiling water and slip off the skins. Slice and sprinkle with lemon juice to prevent discoloring. Force berries through a fine sieve, add the kirsch and sweeten to taste. Whip cream with sugar and vanilla and fold the chilled raspberry puree into the cream. Put the peach slices in serving cups, cover with the whipped cream mixture and chill well before serving.

*If frozen raspberries are used, defrost and strain off the juice before pureeing the berries.

Pineapple Surprise
(for 4 to 6)

1 ripe, unblemished
  pineapple
1 cup strawberries, and
  other fresh fruit in
  season, such as rasp-
  berries, cherries, apricots
  or peaches

½ cup sugar
1 tbsp. lemon juice
1 tbsp. slivered almonds
⅓ cup kirsch

Cut the top off a large pineapple and reserve it. With a sharp knife and spoon cut and remove the flesh of the pineapple, leaving a shell about ½ inch thick. Take care not to pierce the bottom or the sides. Cut out the core of the pineapple and discard. Cut the flesh in cubes, put in a bowl and mix with other diced fruit. Add kirsch, sugar and almonds, mix and let stand for an hour. In the meantime chill the pineapple shell. Then fill the shell with the fruit, cover with the top. Chill it well for at least two hours. For serving stand in a bowl of crushed ice.

Frozen Sabayon
(for 4)

3 egg yolks
2 tbsp. water
4 tbsp. sugar
½ cup dry Marsala wine

1 cup heavy cream,
   whipped
3 tbsp. cognac

Put all ingredients except cream in the top of a double boiler over hot, but not boiling water. Blend and beat this mixture with a wire whisk until it is frothy and warm. Remove from heat and keep on whisking until the mixture is very frothy and has thickened. Fold in whipped cream, pour into a mold and freeze.

Sorbet Deauville
(for 4)

1 pint lemon sherbet
4 tbsp. fresh lemon juice

⅓ cup calvados (or applejack)

Let sherbet soften somewhat, blend in lemon juice and all but 2 tablespoons of the calvados. Refreeze. When serving float a little calvados on top of each individual cup.

Frozen Soufflé
(for 6)

1 cup sugar
1 cup water
8 egg yolks
2 cups heavy cream,
   whipped firm
²/₃ cups candied fruit, diced

1 small pinch of salt
½ tsp. grated orange peel
½ tsp. grated lemon peel
5 tbsp. curaçao liqueur
   blended with 3 tbsp.
cognac

Soak the candied fruit, lemon and orange peel in 2 tablespoons of liquors. Combine water and sugar, boil for a few minutes to make a syrup. Let cool slightly. Beat yolks with a whisk until creamy, and add syrup, while beating. Pour into top of a double boiler, place over simmering water and continue whisking until the mixture is very thick. Place top of double boiler in a bowl with crushed ice, stir mixture until cold. Fold in the whipped cream, the candied fruits and peels and the rest of the combined liquors. Pour into a 1-quart soufflé mold and tie a 3-inch wide strip of oiled paper around the top of the mold since the soufflé will rise above the top of the soufflé dish. Put mold in freezer for at least 4 hours. Before serving, decorate top with a few pieces of candied fruit.

Coffee Bavarian

Prepare a basic Bavarian Cream *(p. 155)* and add 2 tablespoons of instant coffee powder to the egg-yolk and sugar mixture.

Pineapple Bavarian

Proceed as in Basic Bavarian Cream *(p. 155),* soak 2 cups of crushed pineapple in 1 cup of dark rum, drain and add fruit to the chilled custard. Use a slightly larger mold and line it, if desired, with lady-fingers.

Vanilla Bavarian

Make a basic Bavarian Cream as above, but add a 6-inch piece of vanilla bean, cut into several pieces to the milk before boiling it. Remove vanilla when the milk has boiled.

Basic Bavarian Cream

(5 cups)

4 eggs, separated
¾ cup sugar
2 cups boiling milk

2 envelopes unflavored gelatin, softened in ¼ cup
cold water
2 cups whipped cream,
lightly sugared

Put the egg yolks into a saucepan, add the sugar and beat the mixture until it is fluffy and almost white. Place pan over very low heat and,
stirring constantly with a wooden spoon, add immediately the boiling
milk. Cook, stirring constantly until the mixture thickens, being careful
not to let it lump. Remove the saucepan from heat before mixture starts
simmering. Strain custard through a fine strainer into a bowl and blend
in the softened gelatin. Set the bowl into a larger one filled with cracked
ice and cool the custard until it is no longer warm, stirring it all the time.
Then fold the stiffly-beaten egg whites into the custard. Keep the bowl of
custard over the ice, stirring occasionally until it is quite cold and on the
point of setting. Then fold in the whipped cream. Rinse an 8-cup Bavarian mold with cold water, pour in the cream and chill for about 6 hours
before unmolding it at serving time.

Crème de Chocolat
(for 4)

4 ounces (4 squares) of
   bittersweet chocolate
2 tbsp. strong coffee
2 large eggs

4 tbsp. rum
4 tbsp. coffee liqueur
½ cup heavy cream,
   whipped

Melt chocolate in top of double boiler over boiling water, add coffee and stir until smooth. Stir in egg yolks, rum and coffee liqueur. Remove from heat and fold in the stiffly beaten egg whites and the whipped cream. Spoon into crème pots or small demi-tasse cups and chill for at least 3 hours until well set.

Strawberry Cream
(for 4)

1 quart strawberries
1¼ cup crème fraîche *(p. 20)*
   or heavy cream
1 egg white, beaten stiff

3 tbsp. sugar
3 tbsp. sugar
2 tbsp. curaçao or Grand
   Marnier liqueur

Hull the berries and reserve about 6 or the biggest ones. Mash the rest through a sieve or foodmill. Add the liqueur and sugar. Whip the cream; when stiff fold in the beaten egg white and then the pureed strawberries. Put on a serving platter and garnish with the reserved whole berries.

Charlotte à la Valentin
(for 6)

3 cups raspberry preserves
3 dozen plain ladyfingers
  (approximately)

¾ cup superfine sugar
4 egg whites

Put the raspberry preserves in a heavy saucepan and cook over low heat, stirring constantly, for about 20 minutes or until they are very thick. Make a round cake of about 7 inches in diameter, by overlapping layers of ladyfingers, sticking them together with the preserves. Leave an empty space in the center and pour some of the preserves carefully into this space. Top with a few ladyfingers and then coat the cake with the remaining preserves.

Put the cake on a gold foil doily on a small round cake tin. Beat the egg whites and gradually add the sugar. Beat until very stiff. Pipe the meringue in decorative swirls onto the top of the cake and around the bottom. Bake it in a preheated 500⁰ oven for just long enough for the meringue to turn pale golden. Remove from oven, cool and chill well before serving.

Note: You may wish to stir two or three tablespoons of kirsch or framboise brandy into the preserves before coating the ladyfingers.

Tarte des Demoiselles Tatin
(for 6)

1 recipe pâté brisée *(p. 143)*   ½ cup butter, softened
⅓ cup granulated sugar   4 to 5 very tart, firm
⅓ cup brown sugar   cooking apples

Roll out the pastry into a 9-inch round, about ¼ inch thick, and set aside. Butter thickly a 9-inch tart pan or pie plate and cover with a layer of ½ cup sugar (granulated and brown mixed). Peel, core and slice the apples quite thick and arrange neatly on top of the layer of sugar. Sprinkle the apples with the remaining sugar and dot with a little butter. Cover the apples with the pastry but do not crimp the sides. Bake in preheated 400⁰ oven for 25 minutes. Unmold upside down on a plate. If the apples have not sufficiently carmelized, run quickly under the broiler until browned.

Index